FOR BREW FREAKS, BEAN GEEKS AND THE SIMPLY CURIOUS ...

INDEPENDENT COFFEE GUIDE

IRELAND

INSIDER'S GUIDE TO SPECIALITY COFFEE SHOPS AND ROASTERIES

www.saltmedia.co.uk
Tel: 01271 859299
Email: ideas@saltmedia.co.uk

Salt Media *Independent Coffee Guide* team:
Richard Bailey, Nick Cooper, Sophie Ellis, Clare Hunt,
Kathryn Lewis, Tamsin Powell, Jo Rees,
Rosanna Rothery, Amy Sargeant, Christopher Sheppard,
Dale Stiling, Mark Tibbles and Selena Young.
Design and illustration: Salt Media

A big thank you to the *Independent Coffee Guide*
committee (meet them on page 136) for their expertise
and enthusiasm, **our headline sponsor** KeepCup **and
sponsors** Almond Breeze, Boundary, Henny & Joe's,
Marco Beverage Systems and Olam.

Coffee shops, cafes and roasteries are invited to be
included in the guide based on meeting criteria set by the
committee, which includes the use of speciality beans,
providing a high quality coffee experience for visitors and
being independently run.

For information on the *Independent Coffee Guides* North,
Midlands and North Wales, Scotland and South West and
South Wales, visit:

www.indycoffee.guide
 🐦 📷 @indycoffeeguide

N°53

CRACKED NUT

CON-
TENTS

While Ireland has always been a pacemaker in Europe's fast-moving speciality scene, 2019 feels like the year in which the Irish contingent has really stepped up the tempo.

From tech innovations transforming the brew bar, to next-level-geeky roasting gadgetry, the baristas, roasters and coffee specialists across the land have journeyed even further in the pursuit of new territories of flavour.

This pursuit of phenomenal caffeine is driven by the community's determination to ensure a fair price is paid to farmers. This year has seen an increase in *real* direct trade projects at roastery level, alongside increasing consumer interest in who grew the beans and where.

At the coffee shop, these developments are yielding more choice than ever. Guest coffee line-ups are growing by the day, after-hours cupping sessions are becoming the norm and knowledge about the coffees' origins is being shared more widely.

There's never been a better time to explore Ireland's exciting speciality scene. We've put in the hours so you don't need to scroll endlessly to track down a good cup, and I hope the guide will lead you to some incredible coffee encounters. We love to follow your adventures, so feel free to share them with us on social.

Here's to another year of good craic and great coffee.

Kathryn Lewis
Editor
Indy Coffee Guides

 **INDYCOFFEEGUIDE**

HOLD ON TIGHT

THIS IS THE REUSE REVO- LUTION

THE ORIGINAL
BARISTA STANDARD
REUSABLE COFFEE CUP

DESIGN YOURS AT
KEEPCUP.COM

THE FUTURE OF COFFEE

The speciality scene is constantly evolving in its collective quest for the ultimate cup of coffee.

From experimenting with processing at origin to diversifying the traditional coffee shop set-up, meet the businesses brewing the future of Irish caffeine culture ...

UV BEAN SCREENING

WHITE STAR COFFEE, BELFAST

Just one dodgy bean can ruin the profile of a coffee and it's this prospect – plus a fierce dedication to roasting incredible coffee – that's driving White Star's adventures in ultra violet

UV DEATH RAY

Bean defects (classed as primary and secondary) are screened for at the washing stations at origin and by the green bean importers who source coffees for indie roasters. But while primary (and some secondary) defects can be detected by eye, secondary defects such as phenolic taste, rio flavour and over-fermentation aren't detectable without the use of specialist equipment.

'Think of it like dropping an apple,' explains White Star co-founder James Price. *'It may look fine on the surface but under the skin it's bruised.'*

Disappointed by roasting great greens only to discover defects once the coffee reached the cupping table, James and business partner Philip Chick decided to do some research. They stumbled upon a study conducted by Illy, which revealed that UV light could be used to detect secondary defects in green beans.

'Philip and I both come from engineering backgrounds and were familiar with UV light being used to detect structural defects and fractures in metals,' says James. *'The crazy thing was that Illy disregarded the paper as they deemed following this course of action too time consuming and therefore not cost effective.'*

Excited by the possibilities, James and Philip began screening beans with hand held UV lights which causes primary and secondary defects to appear as different colours. The results were phenomenal, so much so that every bean at White Star is now screened using industrial-sized UV lights before roasting, making White Star one of just a handful of roasters in the world screening beans in this way.

'WHITE STAR IS ONE OF JUST A HANDFUL OF ROASTERS IN THE WORLD SCREENING BEANS THIS WAY'

'We roast around 500kg of coffee a week so it's a monstrous task,' says James. *'But if we didn't take that time over the crop, we wouldn't be honouring the farmer who grew the coffee or the barista who will brew them.'*

Around three to four per cent of an average lot which passes through the Belfast roastery will be discarded as defective, and some have been closer to 11 per cent.

'The crops we have screened are a lot better to work with: the beans produce a more consistent and cleaner cup profile. We've also been able to reduce the amount of bacteria-infected beans in natural coffees which gives them over-boozy notes, but it's cost us a lot of time and effort,' adds James.

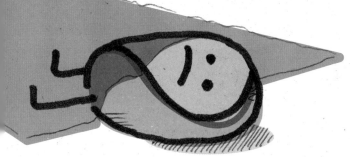

ANAEROBIC FERMENTATION

BAILIES COFFEE ROASTERS, BELFAST

CINNAMON BUN IN A CUP

Just when you thought you'd got your head around the various methods used to process green beans at origin, the innovative team at Bailies go and add a whole extra chapter to the coffee cherry's life story

Traditionally, coffee cherries are picked, sorted (to remove defective beans) and then processed (either washed, natural or honey), before being shipped for roasting.

However the Bailies crew recently met Esteban, a Costa Rican coffee mill owner who's changing the game by introducing an extra step between sorting and processing to encourage anaerobic fermentation of the green beans.

The exact process shifts and adapts with each lot,' explains Bailies' head roaster Stephen Houston. *'Though Esteban's process goes something like this: after sorting, the coffee cherries are placed in a fermentation tank with extra mucilage (the pulpy flesh of the coffee fruit which is removed in washed-process coffees) from other coffee lots of different terroirs, altitudes and varietals.*

'COFFEE THAT TASTES JUST LIKE A CINNAMON BUN'

'The tank is sealed airtight for around 30 hours to allow fermentation. Someone will check and taste the cherries throughout the process to control the fermentation. When the mill owner is satisfied with the taste, the cherries will be processed.'

Why add another – labour intensive – step? Flavour, of course. The bacterial activity of the fermentation process breaks down the sugars within the cherry and unlocks a new level of spice-yielding flavour profiles which can result in coffee that tastes just like a cinnamon bun.

The Bailies gang were so blown away when they tried Esteban's anaerobic-processed coffee that Stephen asked him to use the same process on the beans he would roast for the 2019 World Coffee Championships in Boston.

'There used to be a big focus on natural coffees in competitions,' says Stephen, *'but super rare beans such as Panama geishas could cost around £200 a bag and weren't accessible to the average speciality-savvy coffee drinker.*

'I wanted to roast something that our customers could enjoy too. The La Ortiga beans that I used to compete with were sourced from Esteban's mill within a small community in Tarrazu and are part of our Direct Trade series.'

Currently, anaerobic processing is reserved for high quality coffees, with most of the experimentation happening in mills such as Esteban's in Central America where the coffee communities are in a better financial position to take risks with their crops.

'Hopefully we'll see more countries introducing anaerobic fermentation once it becomes less risky,' adds Stephen. *'It's certainly something we're excited to keep working with at Bailies.'*

COFFEE SHOP/BAR CROSSOVERS

FIRST DRAFT COFFEE & WINE, DUBLIN

COFFEE MEETS WINE

Cafes and bars are pretty much synonymous on the continent, with early morning brews rolling into late night drinks – and it's this relaxed set-up which Ger O'Donohoe has introduced at his Portobello venue

Grab a late afternoon espresso at a coffee shop in most European cities and it's likely that fellow visitors will be quaffing craft beers and carafes of wine while picking over small plates of locally sourced morsels. We've long fetishised this approach and now it's coming to Ireland, thanks to First Draft.

I wanted to create a modern take on traditional European cafe culture,' explains Ger, *'a third space where you can grab a coffee and croissant in the morning, and a glass of wine and something good to eat in the evening.'*

With business rates rocketing and rents following suit, extended opening hours and a wider offering doesn't just benefit the local community looking for a late-night hangout. Creating additional revenue streams and making use of the space after hours can enable small businesses to significantly top up their takings.

'THE MARRIAGE OF SPECIALITY COFFEE AND ORGANIC WINE WAS A NATURAL PAIRING'

'It's a case of adapt or die,' says Ger. *'Rates are crazy in Dublin and will only get worse. The average coffee shop isn't making a lot*

of money – if you're lucky you're covering wages and rent. If you close at four or five, there are another four or five hours when you could be serving customers.'

The marriage of speciality coffee and organic wine at First Draft was a natural pairing for the career barista.

'People who appreciate really good coffee usually feel the same about wine, craft beer and chocolate. Introducing an evening wine list at First Draft allowed me to combine two of my passions,' explains Ger.

'There's definitely a shared language in the wine growing and coffee growing worlds. We curate low-intervention wines created by small producers and love to tell the stories behind the bottles – just like we share tales about the farmers who grow our coffee.'

First Draft's new guise has been a huge success with Portobello locals – so much so that it's usually difficult to score a seat on a Friday or Saturday evening. So can we expect more of our favourite coffee haunts to apply for late licenses?

'In six months time you'll see a lot more cafes going down this route, which I can only see as a good thing,' says Ger.

COFFEE

HOW TO USE THE GUIDE

CAFES

Coffee shops and cafes where you can drink top-notch speciality coffee. We've split Ireland into areas to help you find places near you.

ROASTERIES

Meet Ireland's leading speciality coffee roasteries and discover where to source beans to use at home. Find them after the cafes in each area.

MAPS

Every member cafe and roastery has a number so you can find them either on the area map at the start of each section, or on the detailed city maps.

MORE GOOD STUFF

Discover **More good coffee shops** and **More good roasteries** at the back of the book.

Don't forget to let us know how you get on as you explore the best speciality cafes and roasteries.

🐦 📷 @indycoffeeguide

WWW.INDYCOFFEE.GUIDE

YOUR ADVENTURE STARTS HERE

Nº43

CAMERINO BAKERY

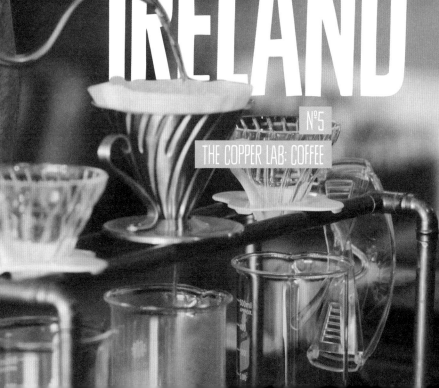

NORTHERN IRELAND

Nº5

THE COPPER LAB: COFFEE

Portrush

Ballycastle

Coleraine

A44

Ballymoney

A37

A26

A29

1

Ballymena

A26

A36

A2

Magherafelt

A26

2

Antrim

M2

3

Lough
Neagh

Newtownabbey

A52

A29

BELFAST
SEE PAGE

Newtownards

A26

38

4

M1

M1

5

A7

Portadown

A1

Ballynahinch

A29

A24

Armagh

Banbridge

A27

6

Warrenpoint

⬢ CAFES

1. Middletown Coffee Co.
2. Linen & Latte
3. Haptik
4. Hollys Coffee Co.
5. The Copper Lab: Coffee
6. Church Lane Coffee

All locations are approximate

MAP 1 MIDDLETOWN COFFEE CO.

60-64 Lower Mill Street, Ballymena, Co. Antrim, BT43 5AF

Stone floors, rustic wooden tables and funky lighting make for a welcoming vibe at this industrial-cool cafe.

The coffee charging the chat includes Dublin-roasted beans from 3FE and a line-up of guests from the likes of Dune, Bonanza and Workshop. Opt for the coffee-tasting set and you can sample all three coffees on the bar that day.

TIP THE TEAM LOVE PLANTS AND CRAFT BEER – FEEL FREE TO QUIZ THEM ON EITHER

No matter how busy it gets, the Marco Jet batch brewer is always ready with a decent filter. *'Good batch brewed filter coffee is the future – but only if it's tasty,'* asserts owner Jonathan Hickinson, who ensures that every batch is tested before serving.

Perch at the window bench and agonise over what to choose from the ever-changing specials such as french toast pimped with seasonal toppings or the eye-popping salted caramel, apple and pistachio cookie sandwich. Everything's cooked in-house and there's a separate plant-based menu too.

ESTABLISHED
2015

KEY ROASTER
3FE

BREWING METHOD
Espresso,
Marco Jet6

MACHINE
Victoria Arduino
Black Eagle
Gravimetric

GRINDER
Victoria Arduino
Mythos One x 2,
Mahlkonig EK43

OPENING HOURS
Mon-Sat
8.30am-**5.30**pm

 Gluten FREE

 BEANS AVAILABLE INSTORE

 WIFI

 CYCLE FRIENDLY

 DISABLED ACCESS

BRING YOUR OWN Cup

COFFEE COURSES

www.middletowncoffee.co   T: 02825 648718

 f @mtowncoffee   @mtowncoffee   @mtowncoffee

MAP №2 LINEN & LATTE

14 Portland Avenue, Glengormley, Newtownabbey, Co. Antrim, BT36 5EY

There are few better ways to start your weekend than savouring really good coffee, tucking into a generous stack of french toast and leisurely browsing homewares. And for Glengormley's lucky locals, that's how Saturdays usually unravel at Linen & Latte.

The charming coffee shop and lifestyle store was an instant hit when it opened in 2015, with its popularity confirmed a few years later when it was crowned Best County Antrim Cafe/Bistro in the Northern Ireland Food & Drink Awards.

VEGGIES AND VEGANS WILL ALSO FIND PLENTY OF FOODIE THRILLS

Kick off brunch with a Bailies flat white (there's also a guest filter from the Belfast roaster) and a serving of the BEST BEANS EVER (cannellini in homemade smoky sauce with sourdough and herby oil dressing). At lunchtime, the brekkie menu is bolstered by gourmet sandwiches, sourdough toasties and specials.

Fully indulged, focus your energy on the curation of books, kitchenware, clothes and more. If you managed self-control over the menu, you'll need a second wind to navigate the shop.

ESTABLISHED
2015

KEY ROASTER
Bailies Coffee Roasters

BREWING METHOD
Espresso, filter

MACHINE
La Marzocco

GRINDER
Mazzer Major On Demand

OPENING HOURS
Tue-Fri **9.30**am-**5**pm
Sat **10**am-**5**pm

 Gluten FREE

 BEANS AVAILABLE INSTORE

 WIFI

 OUTDOOR SEATING

 DISABLED ACCESS

 DOG FRIENDLY

www.linenandlatte.com T: 02890 841518

f @linenandlatte @ @linenandlatte

№3 HAPTIK

29 Frances Street, Newtownards, Co. Down, BT23 7DW

You *could* just drop into Haptik for a grab-and-go, but the opportunity to linger in this Oz-influenced cafe and gallery is really too tempting to turn down.

Eat and drink downstairs where it's all bare brick walls, scrubbed wood and laid-back, airy atmos. Then (expertly poured cappuccino in hand) pop up to the exhibition space to muse over the collection of contemporary works from local artists.

The house roast comes courtesy of Bailies and prep ranges from V60 to french press and batch brew. A gallery of frequently changing guests, including Cloud Picker, Dear Green and Girls Who Grind, means there's never a dull moment for returning fans.

TIP GET A SECOND HELPING OF HAPTIK'S GLORIOUS GRUB AT ONE OF ITS REGULAR SUPPER CLUBS

The popularity of Haptik's signature brunch menu with Newtownards' hungry hordes has resulted in the introduction of extra seating upstairs. Visit to tuck into beautifully presented dishes of huevos rancheros and petal-strewn porridge bowls, or grab a slab of something yummy (baked by Belfast's Man Made) if you're stopping by for elevenses.

ESTABLISHED
2014

KEY ROASTER
Bailies Coffee Roasters

BREWING METHOD
Espresso, pourover, V60, french press, batch brew

MACHINE
La Marzocco Linea

GRINDER
Mahlkonig EK43, Mythos One

OPENING HOURS
Mon-Sat **8.30**am-**4**pm

Gluten FREE

BEANS AVAILABLE INSTORE

WIFI

CYCLE FRIENDLY

DISABLED ACCESS

www.wearehaptik.com

f @wearehaptik   @wearehaptik   @wearehaptik

MAP 4 HOLLYS COFFEE CO.

20 Main Street, Ballynahinch, Co. Down, BT24 8DN

Whether swinging by for a coffee to-go on the way to work, or sitting in (and taking time out), Ballynahinch locals have sniffed out the excellent brews and good vibes at Hollys Coffee.

The cheerful team know their beans and are poised to expertly concoct customers' choice of coffee via espresso, V60, Chemex or AeroPress. Preferred espresso blends include Nota from Bailies and Moondust from Bell Lane, and there's always a daily batch brew on the go if you're paying a speedy visit.

TIP THE COMMUNITY VIBE IS CEMENTED BY EVENTS SUCH AS REGULAR WRITERS' SESSIONS

Planning to linger with a filter? Then getting in on the home baking is a no-brainer. Towering tiered cakes, traybakes and biscuits are imaginatively crafted and painstakingly decorated to mini work-of-art status. Beware the brownies – they're known to reduce the unwary to blissed-out puddles.

Extra space can be found in the converted garage, so caffeine-seeking cyclists and dog walkers now have another good excuse to make a detour.

ESTABLISHED
2015

KEY ROASTER
Multiple roasters

BREWING METHOD
Espresso, V60, Chemex, AeroPress, batch brew

MACHINE
La Marzocco GB5

GRINDER
Mahlkonig EK43, Mazzer

OPENING HOURS
Mon-Tue 8am-4pm
Wed-Sat 8am-5pm

 Gluten FREE

 BEANS AVAILABLE / INSTORE

 WIFI

 CYCLE FRIENDLY

 OUTDOOR seating

 DISABLED ACCESS

 BRING YOUR OWN CUP

 COFFEE COURSES

 DOG FRIENDLY

www.hollyscoffeeco.com   T: 02897 228070

f @hollyscoffeeco   @hollyscoffeeco   @hollyscoffeeco

‡5 THE COPPER LAB: COFFEE

91 Newry Street, Banbridge, Co. Down, BT32 3EF

Photo: Iain Iwrin

Science is both fun and delicious at The Copper Lab, where the chemistry kit includes V60, AeroPress, Chemex and a precision-in-every-pour La Marzocco espresso machine. And the lab technicians weighing up the variables in each superlative cup are brother and sister Stephen Sterritt and Rebecca Równy.

Even the best extraction techniques can be thwarted by poor-quality coffee, which is why the team rely on speciality stalwarts Bailies. Customers, meanwhile, can carry out their own taste experiments via a roster of guest roasters which includes The Good Coffee Cartel and Strangers Coffee Company (with new additions coming soon).

Sourdough, pancakes and porridge inveigle most to hang around for breakfast or brunch, but it's the specials like Swine and Dine (barbecued pulled pork and 'slaw in a brioche bun with loaded spuds on the side) that have wow factor.

‡TIP DON'T MISS THE EVENING WHISKEY AND GIN TASTING SESSIONS

Want to create your own kitchen lab? Attend the team's regular barista evenings and coffee cuppings.

ESTABLISHED
2018

KEY ROASTER
Bailies Coffee
Roasters

BREWING METHOD
Espresso, V60,
batch brew,
AeroPress,
Chemex

MACHINE
La Marzocco
FB80

GRINDER
Victoria Arduino
Mythos One,
Mahlkonig
Tanzania

OPENING HOURS
Mon-Wed, Sat 8am-5pm
Thu-Fri 8am-9pm

www.thecopperlabcoffee.com

f @thecopperlab 🐦 @thecopperlab 📷 @thecopperlab

MAP 6 CHURCH LANE COFFEE

32 Church Street, Warrenpoint, Co. Down, BT34 3HN

Speciality coffee and contemporary Mexican food are difficult enough to locate in big cities, so to find micro-lot filters and seasonally-stuffed burritos on a single menu in a small seaside town is all a bit exciting.

To exceed visitors' expectations with their international set-up was Paddy Goodfellow and Dan Fearon's plan when they launched Church Lane last year. The Bailies house roast and line-up of guest beans from indie roasters (Origin, Caravan and The Good Coffee Cartel to name a few) represent the global coffee-growing belt, while the cooking adds Latin American sizzle. Try the chorizo frittata or stonking pulled-pork burrito bowl to bring a little *¡ay, caramba!* to your lunch break at the foot of the Mourne Mountains.

INSIDER'S TIP PAIR YOUR BREW WITH A CHEESECAKE BROWNIE – YES, YOU READ THAT CORRECTLY

Kooky upcycled furniture, botanical wallpaper and colourful cups also add to the cafe's unique character. Grab one of the bar stools and watch the baristas pull espresso and fashion filters, or nab a comfy chair for more extended lounging.

ESTABLISHED
2018

KEY ROASTER
Bailies Coffee Roasters

BREWING METHOD
Espresso, batch brew, filter

MACHINE
Kees van der Westen Mirage

GRINDER
Mazzer Luigi

OPENING HOURS
Mon-Sat 8am-10pm
Sun 10am-10pm

www.churchlanecoffee.co.uk T: 02841 773606
@churchlanecoffee @churchlanecafe @church_lane_coffee

REW
2.70
BELFAST
GUILT TRIP
PRE ORDER
PAID
PAY ON COLLECTION
NAME
PICK-UP

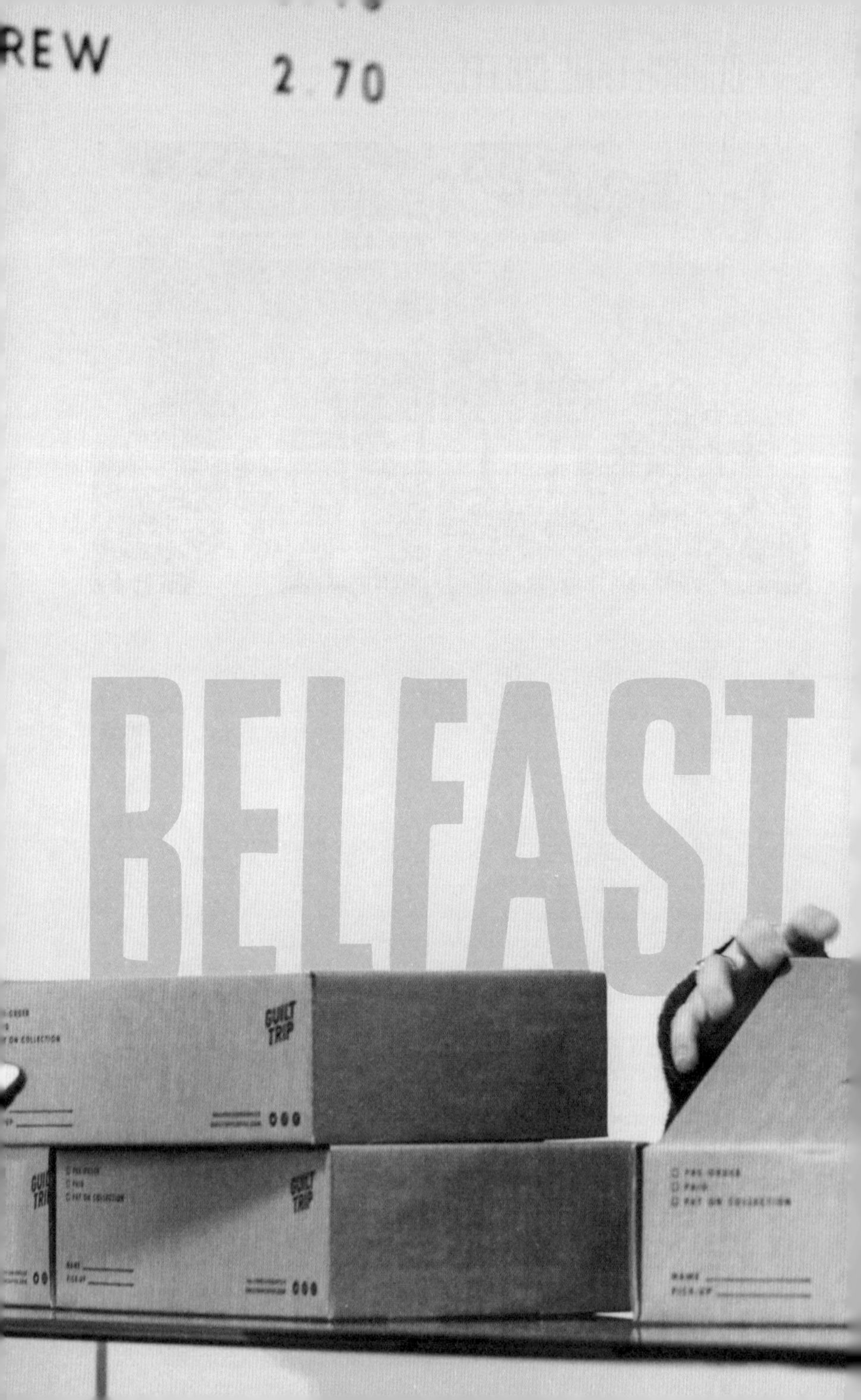

BOX OF 6   12 00

GUILT
TRIP

BELFAST

⬢ CAFES

⬢ ROASTERIES

All locations are approximate

MAP № 7 CURATED KITCHEN & COFFEE

60 Donegall Street, Belfast, BT1 2GT

Salivated over the images of churro french toast with burnt orange caramel in your copy of *Delish: Eat Like Every Day's The Weekend* – but never actually made it? Not got around to sourcing the spices required for Gizzi Erskine's lamb shawarma wrap? We hear you – and we've found a solution.

Curated Kitchen & Coffee not only stocks a hefty library of leading cookery books, it also builds its weekly changing menu around the dishes featured in them, so you can indulge in the delights you've previously only drooled over.

Working on the premise that customers who are fussy about food will also be particular about coffee, owner Alan Cahoon has picked local roaster Root & Branch for the house roast, while also showcasing guests such as Coutume, Redemption, La Cabra and Drop.

INSIDER'S TIP THE TEAM BAGGED BEST CAFE IN COUNTY ANTRIM AT THE IRISH RESTAURANT AWARDS 2019

Inspired by Sydney-cafe guru Bill Granger, Alan's Belfast hangout is big on brunch (served until 3pm, so no excuses) and you can even swoon over Granger's books while munching.

ESTABLISHED
2018

KEY ROASTER
Root & Branch
Coffee Roasters

BREWING METHOD
Espresso, filter

MACHINE
Slayer Steam,
Marco SP9

GRINDER
Victoria Arduino
Mythos One

OPENING HOURS
Mon-Fri 8am-4pm
Sat 9am-4pm
Sun 10am-4pm

 Gluten FREE

 BEANS AVAILABLE INSTORE

 WIFI

 DISABLED ACCESS

 BRING YOUR OWN Cup

 DOG FRIENDLY

www.curatedkitchen.co.uk
f @crtdktchn @crtdktchn

MAP №8 ESTABLISHED COFFEE

37 Talbot Street, Belfast, BT1 2LD

If expertly selected, ground and brewed coffee served in slick surrounds is your thing, the knowledgeable bunch at Established are more than happy to oblige. They are the 2017 and 2018 NI AeroPress champs, after all. And with espresso, V60 and Chemex also at their disposal, there's not much they can't muster.

Roasting duties have been taken in-house this year and Established's seasonal single origins now stock the main grinder and retail shelves. A well-populated roster of international guests (Origin, 3FE, Populus and La Cabra among others) opens up the options via a second grinder.

 KEEP YOUR EYES PEELED FOR THE POP-UP COFFEE KIOSK, JUST ACROSS THE ROAD

Expertise isn't restricted to the baristas, either, as the kitchen offers an epic range of sweet and savoury breakfast and lunch plates. Schedule a Sunday trip to sample the now legendary pie-and-drip combo where awesome bakes are paired with lip-smackingly good coffee.

Brewing and barista courses also run regularly.

ESTABLISHED
2013

KEY ROASTER
Established Coffee

BREWING METHOD
Espresso, batch brew, AeroPress, V60, Chemex

MACHINE
La Marzocco KB90

GRINDER
Mythos One, Mahlkonig EK43

OPENING HOURS
Mon-Fri 7am-6pm
Sat 8am-6pm
Sun 9am-6pm

 Gluten FREE

 BEANS AVAILABLE INSTORE

 WIFI

 DISABLED ACCESS

 COFFEE COURSES

www.established.coffee T: 02890 319416

 @establishedcoffee @established @establishedcoffee

HERE TO HELP YOU GROW

Olam
Specialty
Coffee

Tel: +44 (0) 151 498 6500
Email: osceurope@olamnet.com
olamspecialtycoffee.com

BULLITT

40a Church Lane, Belfast, BT1 4QN

This urban hotel isn't the easiest to find in city centre Belfast, but look out for the archway on bustling Church Lane and you'll soon find yourself in a tranquil oasis of cool design – which also happens to have speciality coffee on tap.

The Coffee Dock espresso bar takes centre stage on the open-plan ground floor and is flanked by the Taylor and Clay restaurant and an outdoor seating area. Above, three floors of contemporary hotel rooms are topped with a swanky rooftop bar.

TIP ASK THE BARISTAS WHICH SPECIAL MICRO-LOTS ARE TUCKED AWAY BEHIND THE BAR

Bailies provides the raw materials for a range of coffee serve styles, and a Brazilian house roast is supported by regularly changing single origins and micro-lot filters, all roasted just across the city.

On Sunday mornings, dirty stop-outs can swing by for their 7am pick-me-up as Bullitt is one of the few Belfast coffee stops open super early on the weekend. And with breakfast available too, it's worth staying out for.

ESTABLISHED
2016

KEY ROASTER
Bailies Coffee Roasters

BREWING METHOD
Espresso, V60

MACHINE
Kees van der Westen Spirit

GRINDER
Victoria Arduino Mythos One

OPENING HOURS
Mon-Sun 7am-late

www.bullitthotel.com   T: 02895 900600

f @bullittbelfast   🐦 @bullittbelfast   📷 @bullittbelfast

MAP 10 FRANKLIN AND JAMES ESPRESSO BAR

Bedford House, Bedford Street, Belfast, BT2 7FD

Franklin and James is the definition of an insider's find: it's almost totally hidden away within the iconic Bedford House building in the heart of Belfast's business district.

Don't feel you can't pass over the threshold, however. Simply glide through the glass front doors, past the friendly chap on reception and swing left to take the steps up to the mezzanine level.

As a specialist Bailies outpost, Franklin and James serves the roastery's espresso (which changes every three months) and a decaf alongside four filters at any time.

TIP SWING BY FOR THE £5 COFFEE AND SANDWICH DEAL BETWEEN 12PM AND 2PM

These are prepared on individual Marco SP9 single-serve brewers which guarantee filter consistency and adorn the counter with their striking profiles.

The space itself is very mid-century modern, and tables are crammed with suited business folk powering up for their next negotiation with peanut balls and Bailies brews – think Mad Men with coffee instead of bourbon.

Sandwiches and scones feature too, but lunch is for wimps, right?

ESTABLISHED
2015

KEY ROASTER
Bailies Coffee Roasters

BREWING METHOD
Espresso, Clever Dripper

MACHINE
La Marzocco Linea PB

GRINDER
Mahlkonig EK43, Mazzer Major

OPENING HOURS
Mon-Fri 7am-4pm

Gluten FREE

WIFI

CYCLE FRIENDLY

DISABLED ACCESS

T: 083 1061070

f @franklinandjamesespressobar @ @franklin_and_james

MAP 11 GUILT TRIP COFFEE + DONUTS

2-4 Orangefield Lane, Belfast, BT5 6BW

More NY than NI, this design-led multi-roaster coffee and donut shop is a deliciously unlikely find on a suburban corner in Belfast.

Unless you're lucky enough to be a local, you're going to have to make a trip – but believe us, you really DO need to make a trip. It's not every day that you find the classic combo (coffee and donuts) at this high quality, so when you get the chance, the only sensible approach is to get stuck in.

TIP THE GUYS DELIVER WITHIN THE BELFAST AREA – A LITTLE KNOWLEDGE IS A DANGEROUS THING ...

Pick from plant-based confections or go full carnivore with a glazed maple and bacon ring. Stumped by having to choose just one from the daily changing selection (all made next door)? You may be looking at a Stay Hungry 12-box.

Switching up the roaster every six weeks or so gives head barista Ben the opportunity to explore all manner of profiles and take punters on flavour adventures in coffee that are as intoxicating as the incredible dough. Recent faves include Assembly and Five Elephant.

ESTABLISHED
2017

KEY ROASTER
Multiple roasters

BREWING METHOD
Espresso, V60, batch brew, AeroPress

MACHINE
La Marzocco Linea PB

GRINDER
Mythos One

OPENING HOURS
Tue-Sat **10**am-**4**pm
Sun **12**pm-**4**pm

 BEANS AVAILABLE INSTORE

 WIFI

 CYCLE FRIENDLY

 OUTDOOR SEATING

 BRING YOUR OWN cup.

www.guilttripcoffee.com T: 07377 532022

f @guilttripcoffee 🐦 @guilttripcoffee 📷 @guilttripcoffee

BELFAST
ROASTERIES

MAP 12 WHITE STAR COFFEE

13 Fountainville Avenue, Belfast, BT9 6AN

Hidden away just off Lisburn Road is one of Belfast's most innovative coffee projects. You'd never even suspect that the half-lab, half-roastery was there unless, on wandering by, you happened to spot purple UV light leaking through the shutters, or a bit of coffee kit through one of the windows.

James Price and Philip Chick created their hideaway HQ as a spot in which to roast small batches of interesting (often experimental) micro-lot beans on their big and little Giesens – while simultaneously pushing the science of coffee.

The team use UV light to screen green beans (some defective beans can only be identified under UV), which is labour-intensive work.

'THE TEAM USE UV LIGHT TO SCREEN GREEN BEANS (SOME DEFECTIVE BEANS CAN ONLY BE IDENTIFIED UNDER UV)'

And while there is immediate benefit in being able to remove duff beans from the batch about to be roasted, the second (and long-term) benefit comes from feeding information back to the growers about the number of defective beans. This helps small-scale farmers produce very high quality (and therefore high value) coffee which will, in turn, improve their quality of life.

ESTABLISHED
2017

ROASTER
MAKE & SIZE
Giesen W15,
Giesen WPG1

OPEN
BY APPOINTMENT

BEANS
AVAILABLE
ONLINE

www.whitestar.coffee   T: 07484 174099

@whitestarcoffee

Nº7

CURATED KITCHEN & COFFEE

MAP№13 BAILIES COFFEE ROASTERS

Unit 1, 27 Stockman's Way, Belfast, BT9 7ET

Sourcing takes as high a priority as roasting at NI's first and only official SCA Premier Training Campus. As a result, the team have been on a mission to define what 'direct trade' really means, labelling appropriate bags of beans with a discreet 'DT' so that coffee fans can identify the real deal.

For Bailies this means not using a middleman but transferring money directly into the pockets of the coffee growers they work with. *'Honouring the skilled labour of farmers and treating them fairly is one of the cornerstones of Bailies' mission,'* says green coffee buyer Jan Komarek. *'Fostering ethical, sustainable and long-term relationships with some of the world's best coffee farmers dovetails with our roasting quest to bring out the distinctive flavours in each coffee.'*

ESTABLISHED
1993

ROASTER
MAKE & SIZE
Probat Neptune 500 120kg,
Probat UG22 22kg,
Probatone 5 5kg,
Probat BRZ 2 100g,
Probat BRZ 5 100g

OPEN
BY APPOINTMENT

COFFEE
COURSES

COURSES

BEANS
AVAILABLE

ONLINE

'THE ROASTERY IS HOME TO NORTHERN IRELAND'S FIRST AND ONLY OFFICIAL SCA PREMIER TRAINING CAMPUS'

They've certainly got the skills to fulfil their ambitions: head roaster Stephen Houston took first place in the Irish Brewers Cup using the roastery's directly sourced Costa Rican El Diamante, and in April represented Ireland in the world comp. Discover the seasonal line-up of coffees at speciality shops across Belfast and beyond.

www.bailiescoffee.com T: 02890 771535

f @bailiescoffee 🐦 @bailiescoffee 📷 @bailiescoffee

REPUBLIC OF IRELAND

Nº29

COACH HOUSE COFFEE

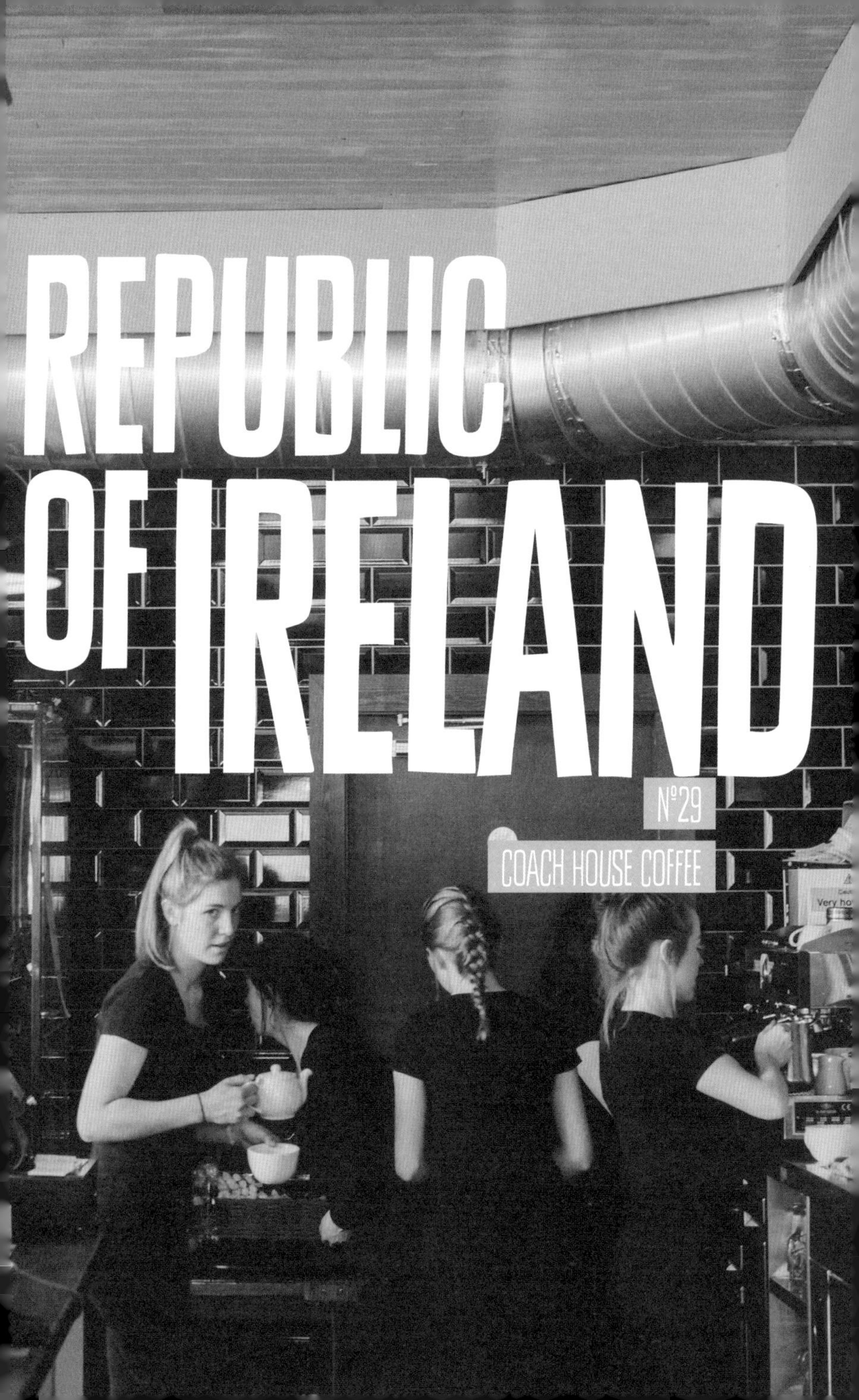

⬡ CAFES

⬡ ROASTERIES

All locations are approximate

MAP 14 THIS MUST BE THE PLACE

High Street, Westport, Co. Mayo, F28 Y440

Ask the crew at this Westport cafe who roasted the beans in your flat white, who picked the leaves garnishing your sweet-potato cakes or who kneaded the sourdough with which you mopped up every last drop of curry mayo and, nine times out of ten, they'll have a name for you.

Championing local producers is at the heart of Susan Timothy and Andrew McGinley's teeny coffee shop, their passion for provenance singing from the inventive, organic and mostly-vegetarian menu. It's one of the reasons customers congregate here for hearty breakfast plates and lunch dishes.

 THE CHILDREN'S EASEL FEATURES 28 YEARS OF KIDS' PAINTINGS FROM SUSAN'S MUM'S PLAYSCHOOL

The coffee receives equal care: it's sourced from Anam in the Burren and skilfully prepared as espresso and pourover.

Live like a true TMBTP local and pair your flat white with the courgette and pistachio dessert. The gluten-free almond brownie is another winner – though good luck getting your mitts on one before they sell out.

ESTABLISHED
2018

KEY ROASTER
Anam Micro Coffee Roastery

BREWING METHOD
Espresso, Chemex, V60

MACHINE
Faema E78

GRINDER
Anfim Super Caimano

OPENING HOURS
Mon-Fri 9am-5.30pm
Sun 10am-4pm

 Gluten FREE

 BEANS AVAILABLE INSTORE

 WIFI

CYCLE FRIENDLY

OUTDOOR SEATING

 BRING YOUR OWN Cup.

 DOG FRIENDLY

T: 087 7074500

f @thismustbetheplacewestport 🐦 @tmbtp_westport @thismustbetheplace_westport

MAP № 15 CAFE LOUNGE

Unit 3, Mercantile Plaza, Carrick-on-Shannon, Co. Leitrim, N41 X472

You know you'll be sipping some of the freshest coffee around when your neighborhood cafe also owns a local roastery. So a lip-smackingly fresh brew is guaranteed at this Carrick-on-Shannon hybrid.

What started as a childhood taste for great coffee escalated into a full-blown career for owner Georgia Visnyei who, after a year of roasting in her kitchen, opened a cafe in which to brew her beans. The Cafe Lounge house blend was such a hit with the public that she launched her roastery, Art of Coffee, soon after.

TIP VISITORS WITH A REUSABLE CUP SAVE 20c ON TAKEAWAY DRINKS

A line-up of ten single origins and blends from across the globe appeals to picky palates and finely-tuned tastes. If you find the selection mindboggling, start with the Lounge blend before exploring something more nuanced such as the Papua New Guinea single origin via cafetiere. Discovered a new favourite? The team roast 1kg bags of coffee to order.

ESTABLISHED
2010

KEY ROASTER
Art of Coffee

BREWING METHOD
Espresso,
cafetiere

MACHINE
Futurmat

GRINDER
Q10, Mahlkonig,
Eureka

OPENING HOURS
Mon-Fri 9am-6pm
Sat-Sun 10am-6pm

Gluten FREE

BEANS AVAILABLE
INSTORE

 WIFI

 OUTDOOR seating

 DISABLED ACCESS

 BRING YOUR OWN Cup.

www.cafelounge.ie   T: 071 9650914
f @cafelounge   @cafeloungecarrickonshannon

MAP № 16 ARIOSA COFFEE

1 Laurence Street, Drogheda, Co. Louth

With its front windows thrown open and the seductive scent of coffee wafting from the La Marzocco Strada, Ariosa proves irresistible to Drogheda's passing coffee boffs. The mother roastery, a mere 20km away, is where the magic begins, with top-quality beans roasted in small batches to tickle out every last drop of flavour.

At the cafe, stonking brews are crafted by uber-friendly baristas who know their stuff. The latest single origins are explored on AeroPress while a shiny new Trinity One offers cold drip opportunities. Don't sweat it if you're a newbie to the brewing basics as the short, sweet and gimmick-free menu keeps things simple.

TIP THERE ARE A COUPLE OF SEATS UNDER THE AWNING FOR SIPPING IN THE SUNSHINE

Toothsome cakes and buttery pastries are on hand to fortify any coffee break, with daily-special sandwiches doing lunchtime service. Ariosa's winning mantra is 'good coffee, good food and good service', and when the sun's over the yardarm, the chance to indulge in a glass of prosecco is thrown into the mix too.

ESTABLISHED
2017

KEY ROASTER
Ariosa Coffee

BREWING METHOD
Espresso,
AeroPress,
Trinity One

MACHINE
La Marzocco
Strada EP

GRINDER
Mythos x 2

OPENING HOURS
Mon-Sat 8am-5pm

 Gluten FREE

 BEANS AVAILABLE INSTORE

 WIFI

 CYCLE FRIENDLY

 OUTDOOR SEATING

DISABLED ACCESS

 BRING YOUR OWN Cup

COFFEE COURSES

 DOG FRIENDLY

www.ariosacoffee.com   T: 085 1455547

f @ariosa.coffee   @ariosacoffee   @ariosacoffee

⚡17 COPPER & STRAW

70 Main Street, Bray, Co. Wicklow, A98 P3F6

Only single origin beans that meet the exceedingly high standards of Copper & Straw founders Stephen and Marcin make the cut at this Bray coffee shop. And it's a policy which is clearly paying off as the cafe bagged a place on *The Irish Times'* Top 50 Coffee Shops list within a month of opening.

The clean-lined space (all high ceilings, house plants and statement tiles) is a tranquil spot where you can watch Stephen working his magic at the reclaimed-wood brew bar. He's usually got five coffees on the go at any time: two for espresso and three for filter (prepared as batch brew or pourover).

TIP THE GUEST ROAST CHANGES MONTHLY AND YOU CAN ALSO PICK UP BEANS TO BREW AT HOME

Bailies provides the house coffee which is regularly joined by guests such as Barcelona's Nomad, Berlin's 19grams and Cornwall's Origin.

Marcin looks after the food offering and is building a following for house specials (which reference his Polish heritage) such as the three cheese toastie with soured cucumbers, and salt beef with sauerkraut.

ESTABLISHED
2018

KEY ROASTER
Bailies Coffee Roasters

BREWING METHOD
Espresso, batch brew, cold brew, V60, Chemex

MACHINE
La Marzocco Linea PB

GRINDER
Mythos One Clima Pro, Mahlkonig EK43

OPENING HOURS
Mon-Fri **7.30**am-**5**pm
Sat-Sun **9**am-**5**pm

 @copperandstraw @copperandstraw

INDY CAFE COOKBOOK

Create a slice of cafe culture at home

food
insider's guide

40 recipes from the kitchens of some of the best speciality coffee shops and roasteries in Ireland and the UK

€25/£20. *Get your copy now at*

WWW.INDYCOFFEE.GUIDE

MAP 18 PS COFFEE ROASTERS

Unit 1, Poplar House, Poplar Square, Naas, Co. Kildare

Sun shining? Grab a cold brew and tonic. Drizzly day? A warming ruby mocha (made from red cacao beans) or a comforting turmeric latte will hit the spot.

Whatever the elements (and your mood), there's a drink to complement at this County Kildare favourite, which was set up by brew-obsessed bros Peter and Simon McCormack.

All the coffee served at PS is roasted at the chaps' new roastery HQ in Clane, where they use green beans sourced from ethical coffee farms across the globe.

 TIP QUIRKY LATTE ART INCLUDES CUTE TEDDY BEARS

In addition to winning brews, the cafe has turned burritos into a veritable art form, offering customers an array of interesting fillings. Like your Tex-Mex super spicy? Take up the hot burrito challenge.

Peter's penchant for good nutrition influences a menu that also offers vegan options like the falafel burger with hummus, and protein ball bites.

ESTABLISHED
2016

KEY ROASTER
PS Coffee Roasters

BREWING METHOD
Espresso, V60, AeroPress, Clever Dripper, french press, syphon

MACHINE
Conti

GRINDER
Mahlkonig EK43, Mythos One

OPENING HOURS
Mon-Fri **8**am-**7**pm
Sat **9**am-**7**pm
Sun **10**am-**6**pm

 Gluten FREE

 BEANS AVAILABLE INSTORE

 WIFI

 CYCLE FRIENDLY

 OUTDOOR seating

 DISABLED ACCESS

 BRING YOUR OWN cup

 COFFEE COURSES

 DOG FRIENDLY

www.pscoffeeroasters.com T: 086 3982467

f @pscoffeeroasters 🐦 @pscoffeeroaster @ @pscoffeeroasters

MAP № 19 SQUARE

Unit 3, Market Square, Kildare, Co. Kildare, R51 NA02

With its monochrome colour scheme and bold typography, this small-town coffee shop could easily pass for a hip city espresso bar.

Inside, a brew bar stocked by local micro-roasters and a menu mainlining Irish produce reveal its true location at the heart of Kildare. Founders Pam and Alan are passionate about their community and, in addition to supporting regional producers, exhibit local artwork and host music and comedy events.

TIP CHECK OUT SQUARE'S NEW SPACE AT CURRAGH RACECOURSE

Beans for the house roast are sourced from the PS Coffee brothers and make a weekly 20 mile trek from the Clane roastery. Guest coffees are usually fairly local too – recent residencies include Bean in Dingle, West Cork Coffee and Galway's Calendar Coffee.

Sink an espresso and a slice of chocolate and stout loaf cake before browsing the thoughtfully curated retail selection. Design-led homewares, contemporary crafts and brewing paraphernalia all feature.

ESTABLISHED
2017

KEY ROASTER
PS Coffee Roasters

BREWING METHOD
Espresso, V60, cold brew

MACHINE
Conti X-One

GRINDER
Nuova Simonelli Mythos One x 2, Mahlkonig Tanzania

OPENING HOURS
Mon-Fri **7.30**am-**5**pm
Sat **9**am-**4**pm
Sun **10**am-**4**pm

 Gluten FREE

 BEANS AVAILABLE INSTORE

 WIFI

 CYCLE FRIENDLY

 OUTDOOR seating

 BRING YOUR OWN cup

 DOG FRIENDLY

www.squarecoffee.ie   T: 087 6157121

f @squarekildare   @squarekildare   @squarecoffee

20 THE PANTRY CAFE & WALLED GARDEN

13 Market Square, Main Street, Portlaoise, Co. Laois

There's an upbeat, happy vibe at The Pantry. It's unsurprising given that it has all the ingredients required for an outstanding coffee experience: exceptional espresso and batch brew, expertly crafted bakes and the warmest welcome rolled out by a smiley team.

Beans come from Dublin's 3FE, with regularly changing single origins stepping up for batch brew duty. The cafe's collection of three grinders is testament to the seriousness with which the gang treat coffee and ensures a proliferation of flavours.

Yet while the coffee's great, the food also hits the mark. Everything is homemade and the menu pared back and honest, prioritising flavour over fads.

TEAM PANTRY SCOOPED BEST CAFE IN THE MIDLANDS 103 AWARDS

When the weather's fine, take your goodies outside and find a spot in the walled garden – it's a much-appreciated sanctuary and an excellent bolthole for basking when it's sunny.

ESTABLISHED
2014

KEY ROASTER
3FE

BREWING METHOD
Espresso,
batch brew

MACHINE
Nuova Simonelli
Aurelia II

GRINDER
Nuova Simonelli
Mythos One
Clima Pro,
Eureka Atom,
Mahlkonig
Tanzania

OPENING HOURS
Mon-Fri **8.30**am-**5**pm
Sat **9**am-**5**pm

Gluten FREE

 BEANS AVAILABLE / INSTORE

 CYCLE FRIENDLY

 OUTDOOR seating

 DISABLED ACCESS

 BRING YOUR OWN Cup

MAP 21 THE LITTLE COFFEE HUT

Burlington Business Park, Tullamore, Co. Offaly, R35 H9W8

Speciality pros are known for their ingenuity when it comes to finding unique places to craft quality caffeine, and Mark Smith's security-hut-turned-coffee-shop in Tullamore is no exception.

Burlington Business Park's workforce bid a welcome farewell to scolding americanos and instant coffee the day the Hut rocked up. With a strictly single origin and distinctly seasonal set-up, Mark offers keyboard warriors a kaleidoscope of flavours via his Astoria espresso machine. He even switches up the Silverskin roast every couple of weeks.

TIP NEED A HEALTH HIT? TRY A SHOT OF WHEATGRASS JUICE

If you're swinging by around 1pm, get ready to join the clan of lunch-breakers queuing for steaming toasties stuffed with locally sourced goodies, plus hunks of homemade traybake. Make it a late lunch and you'll have a better chance of scoring one of the alfresco tables from which to savour an espresso and slice of mallow-stuffed rocky road.

One too many coffees? Soothe the caffeine shakes with a CBD-infused Ko Kombucha.

ESTABLISHED
2018

KEY ROASTER
Silverskin Coffee Roasters

BREWING METHOD
Espresso

MACHINE
Astoria

GRINDER
Mahlkonig K30, Mythos One

OPENING HOURS
Mon-Fri 8am-4pm
Sat at Tullamore Food Fayre

T: 087 6927733
@thelittlecoffeehut

TREE BARK STORE

Kilrainey Shopping Centre, Moycullen, Galway, Co. Galway, H91 W3PO

'**C**offee, retail, photo' is the holy trinity emblazoned on the polished window of Galway's speciality powerhouse.

The space is the brainchild of Jeff Warde and Yvonne Chan who, eager to combine their hospitality backgrounds and passions for quality coffee, Irish produce and photography, launched Tree Bark Store in November 2018.

 BEAUTIFUL DAY? TAKE YOUR COFFEE IN THE NEW ALFRESCO SEATING AREA

The sociable hub hums with good vibes. Original artwork adorns the walls, shelves are stacked with unique finds from regional artisans, and communal benches throng with creatives and coffee fiends. There's even a studio for professional (and practising) photographers where Jeff also records podcasts with local artists.

A seasonally switched-up espresso blend from Calendar keeps disciples bang-up-to-date, while the medley of brewing methods offers plenty of options for filter followers. Pair your pick with one of the pastries from the local market.

ESTABLISHED
2018

KEY ROASTER
Calendar Coffee

BREWING METHOD
Espresso,
Kalita Wave,
batch filter

MACHINE
Nuova Simonelli
Aurelia II

GRINDER
Mythos One,
Mahlkonig
Tanzania

OPENING HOURS
Tue-Fri **8**am-**5**pm
Sat **10**am-**5**pm
Sun **11**am-**4**pm

 BEANS AVAILABLE INSTORE

 WIFI

 OUTDOOR SEATING

 DISABLED ACCESS

 BRING YOUR OWN CUP

www.treebarkstore.com T: 086 7279638

f @treebarkstore @ @treebark.store

BE CONTEMPORARY.
STAY TRADITIONAL.

We understand that speed of service is vital. That's why we created our unique & multi award winning chai infusion. Perfectly blended by a barista for a barista.

CAFFEINE FREE

VEGAN FRIENDLY

ALLERGEN FREE

100% NATURAL

HENNY&JOE'S

#1

CHAI

MASALA CHAI INFUSION

(HINDI; MIXED SPICE TEA)

HANDMADE IN BATH

500ML

APPROX 20 SERVINGS

Say hello, we can chat all day!

hello@hennyandjoes.co.uk | @hennyandjoes | hennyandjoes.co.uk

23 MATT'S SANDWICHES

40 Lower Newcastle, Galway, Co. Galway

Dialling in Berlin-roasted beans and fashioning super-duper sandwiches from local ingredients, Matt O'Flaherty and his team have created a one-stop lunch shop which is definitely worth ditching the packed lunch for.

Passersby, rerouted by the waft of hot-from-the-grill sandwiches, find they've hit the jackpot when they discover speciality grade espresso alongside the carby masterpieces.

Coffees from The Barn are regularly switched up: past picks have included the intense peach and jasmine notes of a Guji Ethiopian single origin, and beans from Finca Himalaya in El Salvador (all pear and vanilla undertones).

TIP ON FRIDAYS, ASK FOR THE PASTRAMI ON RYE – TRUST US ON THIS ONE

While the coffee is cracking, the huge board of creative sandwiches is another crowd-puller and recent additions include the Tir da Loch of rotisserie chicken, fresh mozzarella, sundried tomato and basil pesto. Saturday is bagel day – arrive early if you want to bag one.

ESTABLISHED
2018

KEY ROASTER
The Barn

BREWING METHOD
Espresso

MACHINE
La Marzocco Linea PB

GRINDER
Mazzer Major Electronic

OPENING HOURS
Mon-Thu **8**am-**5**pm
Fri **8**am-**4**pm
Sat **10**am-**1**pm

Gluten FREE

BEANS AVAILABLE
INSTORE

 WIFI

 CYCLE FRIENDLY

DISABLED ACCESS

BRING YOUR OWN Cup.

COFFEE COURSES

www.mattssandwiches.ie   T: 091 527880

f @mattssandwichesgalway   @mattssandwichesgalway

MAP № 24 LITTLE LANE COFFEE COMPANY

10 Abbygate Street Upper, Galway, Co. Galway, H91 KD42

After coffee-tasting their way around the country, Jennifer Power and Graham O'Riordan wanted to create their own coffee house where they could celebrate the bounty of extraordinary beans being roasted across Ireland. And the result is this multi-roaster cafe in the heart of Galway.

The duo curate a three-strong filter menu which offers adventurous sippers a choice of beans from up-and-coming Irish roasters. In need of a little guidance about what to choose? Don't worry, the team are well equipped with tasting notes and recommendations.

INSIDER'S TIP THE BEST SEATS IN THE HOUSE (AT THE WINDOW BENCH) ARE WORTH FIGHTING OVER

Fans of the flat white will relish the roasted peanut, milk choc and caramel notes of the Nota house coffee, though the Bailies beans perform equally well when served black.

Whatever your preferred style, pair your brew with one of the huge hunks of rocky road – the gluten-free treats are made by Turtle and Hare Bakery.

ESTABLISHED
2018

KEY ROASTER
Bailies Coffee Roasters

BREWING METHOD
Espresso, V60, pourover

MACHINE
La Marzocco Linea PB

GRINDER
Mahlkonig Tanzania, Mazzer

OPENING HOURS
Mon-Fri 8am-5.30pm
Sat 9am-5.30pm
Sun 10am-5.30pm

 Gluten FREE

 BEANS AVAILABLE INSTORE

 WIFI

 CYCLE FRIENDLY

 OUTDOOR SEATING

 DISABLED ACCESS

 BRING YOUR OWN CUP

 DOG FRIENDLY

MAP № 25 COFFEEWERK + PRESS

4 Quay Street, Galway, Co. Galway

The interior of this Galway coffee shop reveals it's as serious about design as it is about crafting speciality coffee.

But what else would you expect from a cafe which also serves as a lifestyle store and publishing house? Bright white walls, minimalist Scandi design and natural light provide the perfect backdrop to hip coffee sipping.

 TIP GUEST BEANS TOUR THE COFFEE ROASTING WORLD – RECENT RESIDENCIES INCLUDE VANCOUVER'S LUNA

Beans from The Coffee Collective reinforce the European vibe, and seasonal roasts from the Copenhagen outfit capitalise on the clean and bright flavours which typify the Nordic roasting style. If you've got time to spare, sample the latest lot on Kalita filter and explore its unique tasting notes.

There's a small selection of golden pastries to pair with your coffee, as well as a hefty selection of design mags to flick through. The lust-list collection of homewares, kitchen gear and quality cosmetics is also worth browsing.

ESTABLISHED
2015

KEY ROASTER
The Coffee Collective

BREWING METHOD
Espresso, Kalita Wave, cold brew

MACHINE
La Marzocco Linea PB

GRINDER
Mythos One, Mahlkonig EK43

OPENING HOURS
Mon-Fri **8.30**am-**6**pm
Sat-Sun **9**am-**6**pm

 Gluten FREE

 BEANS AVAILABLE INSTORE

 WIFI

 OUTDOOR seating

 BRING YOUR OWN Cup.

www.coffeewerkandpress.com   T: 09 1448667

f @coffeewerkandpress   @coffeewerkpress   @coffeewerkandpress

MAP 26 DOOLIN INN

1 Fisher Street, Doolin, Co. Clare, V95 CC79

Fancy waking up to a cracking cup of coffee at a coastal spot in rural County Clare? That's what happens when you stay the night at Doolin's village inn.

However it's not just overnighters who get to revel in the smug high that comes with imbibing an expertly pulled espresso at this Doolin hub, as the cafe also welcomes day-trippers and locals looking to satiate their speciality cravings.

Beans roasted by Anam travel all of 20 minutes from the Kilcorney roastery to be served as espresso or cafetiere. If the weather's playing ball, grab a spot on the ocean-view terrace and get stuck into the latest brew while acquainting yourself with the tasting notes.

INSIDER TIP MAKE AN EVENING TRIP TO WATCH THE SUN SLIP INTO THE SEA FROM THE FLOOR-TO-CEILING WINDOWS

A stay at the Doolin Inn isn't complete without testing the limits of your gluttony at the breakfast buffet. With a focus on local ingredients such as Burren cheeses, smoked salmon and homemade pastries, your standard hotel continental this ain't.

ESTABLISHED
2012

KEY ROASTER
Anam Micro
Coffee Roastery

BREWING METHOD
Espresso,
cafetiere

MACHINE
Nuova Simonelli
Aurelia II

GRINDER
Mythos One

OPENING HOURS
Mon-Sun 7.45am-9pm

www.doolininn.ie   T: 065 7074421

f @doolininn   @ @doolin_inn

^{MAP №}27 GREEN ONION CAFE

3 Rutland Street, Limerick, Co. Limerick

From the colourful posters, local art and murals, to the chilled midweek blues soundtrack, you've got to admire this friendly and eclectic coffee shop which provides an antidote to Limerick's sea of cafe chains.

When it comes to coffee and food, owner David Corbett certainly knows his onions. Satisfying brunches and lunches with an organic, wholefood and local emphasis (and plenty of vegan options) are much loved by the laid-back Limerick crowd. A San Ignacio blend of Brazilian and Costa Rican beans, roasted by Anam in the Burren, complements perfectly.

GOOD LUCK CHOOSING BETWEEN FOUR DIFFERENT TYPES OF FRESHLY BAKED SCONES

Opt for an intimate tête-à-tête in the inner room (all upcycled American embassy chairs and recycled floorboards) or, for more communal conviviality, grab a seat at the sharing table in the plant-themed rear room.

Want to replenish your home brew bar? The mahogany former bank-counter out front is where locals stock up on bags of beans and brewing equipment, foraged and organic loose leaf teas and homemade bakes.

ESTABLISHED
2018

KEY ROASTER
Anam Micro
Coffee Roastery

BREWING METHOD
Espresso

MACHINE
Gaggia Deco

GRINDER
Macap On
Demand

OPENING HOURS
Mon-Fri **8**am-**5**pm
Sat-Sun **9**am-**4**pm

Gluten FREE

BEANS AVAILABLE

INSTORE

WIFI

CYCLE

FRIENDLY

BRING YOUR OWN
Cup.

T: 061 311889

 @greenonioncafe 🐦 @cafe_onion 📷 @greenonionlimerick

bailiescoffee.com
@bailiescoffee

PREMIER
TRAINING CAMPUS

Barista Training in Northern Ireland

SCA Premier Training **Campus**

Bailies Coffee Barista Training

Qualified AST Barista Trainers

Brewing & Grinding Training

Sensory Skills Training

Barista **Skills** Training **Belfast**

Professional Barista Training

Barista Training?
We've got you covered.

Nº 28 CAKEFACE

16 Irishtown, Kilkenny, Co. Kilkenny

At this Kilkenny gem, the only thing capable of overshadowing the patisserie's spot in the limelight is the flawless latte art on the flat whites.

Thankfully there's no need for rivalry between the baristas and bakers as, once visitors have caught a whiff of the freshly ground beans from a host of Irish roasters and set eyes on the decadent desserts, it takes otherworldly willpower to turn either down.

After successful careers in the kitchens of some of London's best restaurants, founders Laura and Rory Gannon returned home to launch Cakeface. The first phase of the colourful cafe was such a hit that, two years later, they extended into next door, building a development kitchen where passersby can watch the chefs at work.

IT'S NOT ALL SWEET THRILLS – THE SOURDOUGH SANDWICHES ARE PRETTY SPECIAL TOO

A double grinder set-up allows enthusiasts to match a brew to their bake, and a guest option provides filter and AeroPress opportunities. You'll also find beans available to buy and take home from whichever roaster is guesting.

ESTABLISHED
2016

KEY ROASTER
3FE

BREWING METHOD
Espresso, filter, AeroPress

MACHINE
BFC Lira

GRINDER
Mazzer

OPENING HOURS
Mon-Sat 10am-6pm
Sun 10am-4pm

 Gluten FREE

 BEANS AVAILABLE INSTORE

 WIFI

 CYCLE FRIENDLY

 OUTDOOR seating

 DISABLED ACCESS

 BRING YOUR OWN Cup

 COFFEE COURSES

DOG FRIENDLY

www.cakeface.ie T: 056 7739971

f @cakefacepastry @cakefacepastry @cakefacepastry

MAP № 29 COACH HOUSE COFFEE

The Courtyard, The Workhouse, Kilmacthomas, Co. Waterford, X42 VY33

Adventure junkies rejoiced when Coach House Coffee started slinging quality espresso in Kilmacthomas in 2017. The 19th century workhouse-turned-caffeine-hub sits right on the edge of popular hiking and cycling route Waterford Greenway, so in summer expect to join a throng of Lycra groupies and dog walkers catching rays on the outdoor seating.

Dublin-based Java Republic bronzes the Coach House custom blend which forms the chocolatey espresso for the signature flat whites. Tired legs in need of a serious caffeine hit head straight to the filter option where guest roaster Roasted Brown showcases single origin beans.

TIP PLANNING A PARTY? THE PIGEON LOFT DOUBLES AS AN EVENT SPACE

Offering a bird's-eye view over the rustic bar, the new Pigeon Loft eatery on the mezzanine level is another reason to schedule a pit stop. Head chef Shane McGrath has given the menu a refresh to match the new space – fuel up on hearty brunches, open sandwiches and gravity-defying burgers ahead of an afternoon of adventure.

ESTABLISHED
2017

KEY ROASTER
Java Republic

BREWING METHOD
Espresso, filter

MACHINE
La Marzocco
Linea PB

GRINDER
Nuova Simonelli
Mythos One

OPENING HOURS
Mon-Sun 8am-6pm

www.coachhousecoffee.ie T: 051 295654

f @coachhousecoffeeirl 🐦 @chcgreenway @coachhousecoffeeirl

№30 BEAN IN DINGLE

Green Street, Dingle, Co. Kerry

Expect a warm welcome from all generations of the Burgess family when you step over the threshold of Bean in Dingle. This cool spot mixes urban funk and downright friendliness with a disco soundtrack and the sizzle of the steam wand.

Since the cafe's launch in 2015, the ambition to serve top-notch coffee has stepped up another gear and the team now meticulously roast their own beans.

Owners and brothers Justin and Luke, along with roaster Katie, ensure farm-to-cup quality by sourcing fairly traded, in-season beans of the highest cup scores. The house blend harvests from Brazil, Guatemala and Ethiopia to create a chocolate-caramel brew with red berry zing.

TIP ENJOY THE HOUSE BLEND 'TIL LATE IN THE COFFEE STOUT, WHICH IS MADE BY DICK MACK'S BREWHOUSE

Alongside the coffee (espresso, batch, AeroPress and V60) there's plenty of honest-to-goodness food to tuck into. Be quick if you fancy the sound of the pork and black pudding sausage roll, and miss Nan Burgess' baking at your peril.

ESTABLISHED
2015

KEY ROASTER
Bean in Dingle

BREWING METHOD
Espresso, batch brew, cold brew, AeroPress, V60

MACHINE
La Marzocco Linea PB

GRINDER
Mahlkonig Peak, Mahlkonig EK43 S, Mythos One Clima Pro, Anfim Super Caimano

OPENING HOURS
Mon-Sat **8**am-**5**pm
Sun **10**am-**3**pm

www.beanindingle.com T: 086 4009489

 @beanindingle   @beanindingle   @beanindingle

MIX
3 TEMPERATURES
1 WATER BOILER

JET
PRECISION BATCH BREWER

marco

SP9
PRECISION POUR OVER BREWER

FRIIA
❄ COLD ♨ HOT
§ SPARKLING

MARCOBEVERAGESYSTEMS.COM

MAP 31 MY BOY BLUE

Holyground, Dingle, Co. Kerry

This brunchers' paradise on the Dingle Peninsula celebrates its second birthday this year, and the cafe's reputation as *the* place for an incredible feed isn't showing any signs of changing.

Since 2017, locals have traded uninspiring packed lunches for the likes of Thai curry with sweet potato poppadoms, and smoked salmon bruschetta smothered in beetroot and walnut salsa.

TIP PIMP YOUR GRILLED CHEESE WITH GOAT'S CHEESE AND HONEY, RED ONION RELISH OR BLACK PUDDING

Even the classics are given an edgy thrill here: eggs and avocado are ramped up with chilli peanut rayu and plated with Insta-ready precision. The bakes are pretty toothsome too, especially the homemade banana bread.

Founder Stephen enlisted his chums at 3FE to roast the house coffee, and his pared-back drinks bill showcases the complex flavours via espresso and filter. The Momentum blend has taken up residency on the first grinder and stumps up chocolatey, nutty notes as espresso. A second Mythos showcases a revolving line-up of single origins from the Dublin roastery.

ESTABLISHED
2017

KEY ROASTER
3FE

BREWING METHOD
Espresso, Kalita Wave, Chemex

MACHINE
Nuova Simonelli Aurelia

GRINDER
Victoria Arduino Mythos One x 2, Mazzer Major

OPENING HOURS
Mon-Tue, Thu-Sat
8.30am-**5**pm
Sun **9.30**am-**4**pm

Gluten FREE

BEANS AVAILABLE
INSTORE

WIFI

BRING YOUR OWN Cup.

T: 086 8444157

 @myboybluedingle @myboybluedingle

REPUBLIC
OF IRELAND
ROASTERIES

ARIOSA COFFEE ROASTING CO

№32 ART OF COFFEE

Unit 6, The Hive, Carrick-on-Shannon, Co. Leitrim, N41 RY66

The love affair between artists and their favourite cafes is well documented, but architects Georgia Visnyei and Gabor Stefcsik decided to take this relationship to the next level. The creative pair (later joined by roaster and artist Gerry) set up a coffee shop, Cafe Lounge, where they brewed up their own small-scale roasted beans.

Their carefully crafted coffees turned out to be so popular with the locals that the team felt compelled to open a dedicated roastery in the town – and so Art of Coffee (the name refers to their creativity) was born.

ESTABLISHED
2009

ROASTER
MAKE & SIZE
Probatone 12kg,
Probatone 5kg

OPEN
BY APPOINTMENT

BEANS
AVAILABLE
ONLINE

'THE LOVE AFFAIR BETWEEN ARTISTS AND THEIR FAVOURITE CAFES IS WELL DOCUMENTED'

At the roastery, green beans are slowly bronzed on the latest Probat roasters (chosen for their profiling precision and fitted with air filters to improve green creds) which yield intricate flavours from single origins, blends and decafs.

And the creativity doesn't stop once the beans have been bagged. By offering their wholesale clients staff-training and advice on equipment, they ensure their customers are as confident about the art of crafting exquisite coffees as Georgia, Gabor and Gerry.

www.artofcoffee.ie   T: 074 9590120
f @artofcoffeecarrickonshannon @artofcoffeecarrick

MAP № **33** BELL LANE COFFEE

Unit 6-7, The Enterprise Centre, Clonmore, Mullingar, Co. Westmeath

It's all blue skies at Bell Lane thanks to a booming year which has included exhibition success, vibrant new packaging and an inspiring first trip to origin.

To coincide with the launch of the first single origin collection, co-founder Stephen travelled to Honduras with green coffee buyer Niko to kickstart the roastery's direct trade programme. Their first success was a partnership with Amprocal, a female-only co-operative which is part of the International Women's Coffee Alliance.

'EXHIBITION SUCCESS, VIBRANT NEW PACKAGING AND AN INSPIRING FIRST TRIP TO ORIGIN'

In addition to featuring lots from Honduras, the collection of sensational single origins also showcases farms in Ethiopia and Kenya, and can be explored via Bell Lane's subscription service and online shop.

Research and development have also been high on the agenda this year and a new Mill City 500g sample roaster (the first of its kind in Ireland) has allowed the team to create accurate profiles when experimenting with expensive coffees.

Bell Lanes' team of SCA-accredited ASTs continue to share their expertise with budding brewers via training classes and certified barista courses.

ESTABLISHED
2012

ROASTER
MAKE & SIZE
Giesen 30kg,
Giesen 15kg,
Mill City 500g

COFFEE COURSES

COURSES

BEANS AVAILABLE
ONLINE | ONSITE

---

www.belllane.ie T: 044 9390777

f @belllanecoffee 🐦 @belllanecoffee 📷 @belllane_coffee

№34 ARIOSA COFFEE ROASTING CO

Borranstown, Ashbourne, Co. Meath

While you might not expect the green fields of Ireland to be scented with coffee, if you venture into the Ashbourne countryside that may be what you experience. It's here in Ireland's agricultural heartland that you'll find Michael Kelly and his team hard at work bronzing beans.

The coffee used at the County Meath roastery is carefully sourced and bought directly and fairly with an eye on the integrity of the supply chain. Micro-lots are then roasted in either the 15kg Toper or 25kg Probat.

Top-quality equipment operated with skill and precision means that every bag of Ariosa coffee is as good as the last. And an early-week roasting schedule gives beans the chance to rest before they're shipped. Retail customers can make the most of their stash by following Ariosa's super-simple online brew guides.

ESTABLISHED
2003

ROASTER
MAKE & SIZE
Probat 25kg,
Toper Cafemino
15kg

OPEN
BY APPOINTMENT

BEANS
AVAILABLE

'IN IRELAND'S AGRICULTURAL HEARTLAND YOU'LL FIND MICHAEL KELLY AND HIS TEAM BRONZING BEANS'

With around 15 coffees available at any time – from berry-flushed Ethiopians to creamy Peruvians – the Ashbourne roastery is a good starting point for adventures in coffee.

www.ariosacoffee.com   T: 01 8010962

f @ariosa.coffee   🐦 @ariosacoffee   📷 @ariosacoffee

^{MAP №}35 PS COFFEE ROASTERS

Unit 1b, Yew Tree Square, Prosperous Road, Clane, Co. Kildare

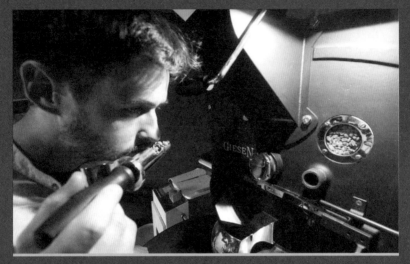

At their family roastery in County Kildare, bean-obsessed bros Peter and Simon McCormack champion ethical sourcing.

'We prefer to work with farmers and importers who adopt a sustainable approach; people who go above and beyond to provide fair pay for farmers and their workers,' says Simon.

They're also fired up about the planet and go the extra mile to be as environmentally friendly as possible.

'WE'RE FOCUSED ON QUALITY – BUT WE AIM HIGHER'

'We offer our wholesale customers discounts when they avail themselves of our reusable containers,' adds Simon.

The pair concentrate on micro batches of high grade single origin coffee which they roast to exacting standards. Their beloved Giesen W15A might be a 15kg capacity machine but they often run smaller batches so they can keep the quality of the roasts tip-top.

'Like many roasters we're focused on quality – but we aim even higher,' adds Simon.

Enjoy the fruits of their labours with a coffee to-go on-site, or pop into the popular Naas cafe.

ESTABLISHED
2015

ROASTER
MAKE & SIZE
Giesen W15A
15kg

CAFE ONSITE

OPEN TO THE PUBLIC

COFFEE COURSES

BEANS AVAILABLE
ONLINE ONSITE

---

www.pscoffeeroasters.ie   T: 083 8022668

f @pscoffeeroasters   🐦 @pscoffeeroaster   📷 @pscoffeeroasters

MAP Nº 36 ANAM COFFEE

Kilcorney, Kilfenora, Co. Clare, V95 YV40

Proving that size really doesn't matter when it comes to creating exquisite coffee, Anam more than punches above its weight.

The County Clare roastery isn't just tiny, it's also remote; set in a windblown valley amid the evocative limestone landscape of the Burren.

The driving force behind Anam is lifelong coffee obsessive Brian O'Briain. Each roast is infused with his passion and benefits from the holy trinity of seasonal sourcing, skilled processing and subtle use of tech.

Proud SCA member Brian is unabashed in stating that he pays a premium for first-rate beans so that traceability and sustainability are ensured – along with game-changing flavours.

'ANAM MORE THAN PUNCHES ABOVE ITS WEIGHT'

Small batches are hand roasted in the custom-built Giesen, while blending happens post-roast and aims to balance taste and body with a hint of sweetness. Single origins are treated with special reverence.

There's also a cracking Mexican Mountain Water decaf (notes of dates, dried fruits and spice) if you're attempting to dial down the caffeine intake.

ESTABLISHED
2017

ROASTER
MAKE & SIZE
Giesen W15,
Giesen W1,
IKAWA sample
roaster

OPEN
BY APPOINTMENT

BEANS
AVAILABLE
ONLINE

---

www.anamcoffee.ie   T: 085 1316665

f @anamcoffee   🐦 @burrencoffee   📷 @burrencoffee

MAP№ 37 THE OLD BARRACKS COFFEE ROASTERY

Birdhill, Co. Tipperary, V94 AX53

Coffee-curious parents have permission to leave the kids at home when they visit this adult-only cafe, roastery and barista training space.

The unique coffee oasis allows grown-ups to get some head space, chat about beans and leisurely choose from up to ten brews. Magical views overlooking the Moylussa mountains and Shannon Lake are conducive to caffeinated good times.

The contemporary coffee experience (an innovative project from Alan Andrews of training and education business, Coffee Culture) offers plenty of inspiration for the coffee fan and cafe owner alike.

'THE UNIQUE CAFFEINE OASIS ALLOWS GROWN-UPS TO GET SOME HEAD SPACE AND CHOOSE FROM UP TO TEN BREWS'

Prop up the bar and witness Europe's only gravimetric Modbar machine in action, catch coffee-roasting demos and chat to experts about everything from sourcing, storing and roasting to cupping, brewing and latte art.

Cupping sessions take place every Sunday morning and there are regular food pop-ups, yoga classes, events and training opportunities, as well as an in-house shop for those who want to recreate the experience at home.

ESTABLISHED
2018

ROASTER
MAKE & SIZE
Giesen W15
15kg

CAFE ONSITE

COFFEE COURSES

COURSES

BEANS AVAILABLE

---

www.theoldbarracks.ie   T: 061 623001

f @theoldbarracks   🐦 @old_barracks   📷 @oldbarrackscoffeeroasters

MAP 38 WCC ROASTERY

The Forge, Innishannon, Co. Cork, T12 W72X

WCC got off to a flying start when it was launched in 2016 as, after just a year in business, its coffee was selected for the London Coffee Masters.

Since the beginning, founder Tony Speight has only allowed seasonal and certified-organic speciality beans to enter the WCC roastery. Samples are test-driven on an IKAWA Pro and Huky 500 before full roasting duties are handed over to the Giesen W6A.

Working with cafe partners to ensure beans hit the mark is central to Tony's quality ethos, and roast profiles are often tweaked to suit the tastes of individual customers.

ESTABLISHED
2016

ROASTER
MAKE & SIZE
Giesen W6A,
IKAWA Pro,
Huky 500

OPEN
BY APPOINTMENT

COFFEE
COURSES

BEANS
AVAILABLE

'A PERCENTAGE OF WCC'S GREEN BEAN COSTS GOES TO INITIATIVES THAT SUPPORT COFFEE FARMERS'

Keeping coffee fair and sustainable is also crucial, so WCC partners with World Coffee Research. That means a percentage of its green bean costs goes to initiatives that support coffee farmers.

The roastery's range roams the globe, and features stonkingly bold and chocolatey Colombians, berry-tinged varieties from Ethiopia and citrusy Peruvian lots. And whichever you choose, Tony will know the back-story.

www.westcorkcoffee.ie T: 086 3183236

@westcorkcoffee   @westcorkcoffee

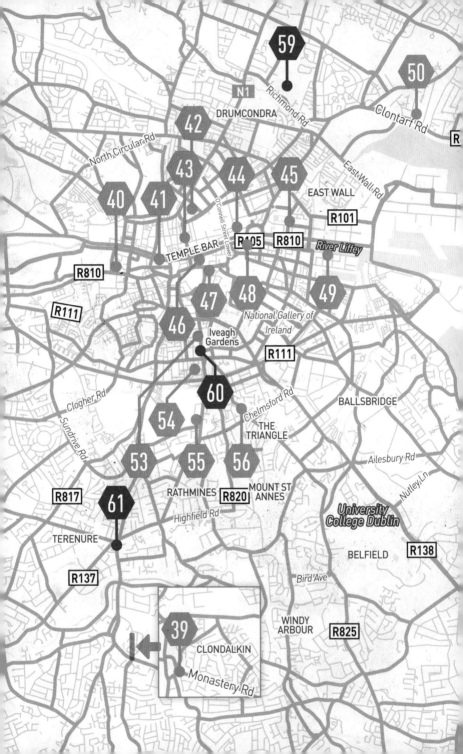

North Bull Island

PORTMARNOCK

R854

52

Strand Rd

◖ CAFES

39	East Village Coffee
40	Container Coffee
41	Craft Coffee Roasters
42	Blas Cafe
43	Camerino Bakery
44	Tang
45	Coffeeangel IFSC
46	Indigo & Cloth
47	Bear Market Coffee
48	Shoe Lane Coffee – Tara Street
49	À Table
50	Ebb & Flow Coffee
51	Happy Out Cafe
52	Honey Honey
53	Cracked Nut
54	First Draft Coffee & Wine
55	Two Fifty Square
56	Project Black
57	Shoe Lane Coffee – Dun Laoghaire
58	Urbun Cafe

⬢ ROASTERIES

59	Upside Coffee Roasters
60	Full Circle Roasters
61	Two Fifty Square Coffee Roasters

All locations are approximate

DUBLIN

Dun Laoghaire Harbour

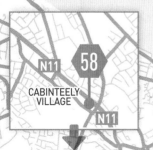

N11

58

CABINTEELY
VILLAGE

N11

N31

57

York Rd

George's St Upper

MAP № 39 EAST VILLAGE COFFEE

Unit 3, Monastery Road, Clondalkin, Dublin 22

Clondalkin's speciality fans have been keeping this homely hangout close to their chests since it opened in 2016. And with its killer playlist, rabble of friendly baristas and daily caffeine pun (courtesy of the wise-cracking sandwich board), it's easy to see why the locals have fallen for its charms.

However, the bewitching waft of freshly ground coffee and straight-from-the-oven scones are scuppering patrons' efforts to keep East Village to themselves. And the cafe's vibrant colour scheme and funky prints don't help, either.

TIP BUY A BAG OF BEANS IN-STORE AND YOU'LL GET A FREE COFFEE TO-GO

Keen to stay current, founder Jonathan Barr recently updated the house roaster and now keeps Clondalkin buzzing with a Full Circle single origin. A new Mythos One also joined the ranks recently to precision-grind a roll call of guest beans from the likes of Urbanity and Upside.

Drop in at lunchtime to check out specials such as the 12-hour pulled-pork brioche bun. #Drool.

ESTABLISHED
2016

KEY ROASTER
Full Circle Roasters

BREWING METHOD
Espresso, AeroPress

MACHINE
Nuova Simonelli Aurelia II

GRINDER
Mythos One, Mahlkonig K30

OPENING HOURS
Mon-Fri 8am-4pm
Sat-Sun 9am-3.30pm

www.eastvillagecoffee.ie   T: 01 4642439
f @eastvillagedub   🐦 @eastvillagedub   📷 @eastvillagecoffee

MAP №40 CONTAINER COFFEE

161 Thomas Street, Dublin 8

Whether it's the call to caffeinated arms chalked on the blackboard outside, or the arresting sight of the bright blue shipping containers, it's certainly difficult to pass Container Coffee without a second glance.

Flagging tourists visiting the Guinness Storehouse (mere minutes away) are lured in by the promise of rejuvenation, while creative types housed in The Digital Hub flock for flatties to-go.

As a small space, it's an espresso-only set-up. Cloud Picker provides the Sam house blend which regularly makes the same journey from the dockyards that the shipping containers did.

THE LINE-UP OF TREATS INCLUDES VEGAN FUDGE FROM LOCAL CAMERINO BAKERY

Time to linger? The outdoor courtyard with its brightly coloured tables and view of St Patrick's Tower is a draw in summer. If you've overdone it on the caffeine (or stout) plump for an iced matcha, chai or turmeric latte. Or, if the weather isn't playing ball, nab an inside seat and hunker down with a sausage roll (there are vegan options, too) or a steaming bowl of porridge.

ESTABLISHED
2017

KEY ROASTER
Cloud Picker

BREWING METHOD
Espresso

MACHINE
Sanremo Verona

GRINDER
Anfim SP II

OPENING HOURS
Mon-Fri
7.30am-5.30pm
Sat 9am-4pm
Sun 10am-4pm

 Gluten FREE

 BEANS AVAILABLE INSTORE

 WIFI

 CYCLE FRIENDLY

 OUTDOOR seating

 DISABLED ACCESS

 BRING YOUR OWN Cup

 DOG FRIENDLY

www.containercoffee.ie T: 087 3513920

f @containercoffeedublin 🐦 @containerdublin @containercoffeedublin

MAP 41 CRAFT COFFEE ROASTERS

27 Merchant's Quay, Dublin 8

If you like using your coffee break as a way to escape the hustle and bustle of city centre Dublin, you'll want to bookmark this little spot.

Located on the banks of the River Liffey and bearing a laid-back vibe, Craft is a welcome (caffeinated) refuge.

Its eclectic soundtrack, collection of movie artwork and quality caffeine have made it a favourite with locals looking for a cosy corner where they can catch up on their latest read, as well as with weekenders in search of time out.

The house blend from Cork Coffee Roasters fuels the page-turning while leisurely lounging is accompanied by a selection of seasonal drinks.

TIP LIKE WHAT YOU'RE DRINKING? PICK UP A BAG OF BEANS TO BREW AT HOME

Join the local workforce for a lunch of freshly stuffed sandwiches and golden pastries, or invest in a KeepCup and take a flattie to-go for a riverside stroll.

ESTABLISHED
2014

KEY ROASTER
Cork Coffee Roasters

BREWING METHOD
Espresso, Moccamaster

MACHINE
La Marzocco

GRINDER
La Marzocco

OPENING HOURS
Mon-Sun 7am-6pm

Gluten FREE

BEANS AVAILABLE
INSTORE

WIFI

BRING YOUR OWN Cup

---

www.craftcoffeeroasters.ie   T: 01 5380040

f @craftcoffeeroasters   @ @craftcoffeeroasters

MAP 42 BLAS CAFE

26 Kings Inns Street, Dublin 1

For five years, Blas' bright and airy space has hosted sociable lunches and coffee catch ups.

In a former life the backstreet building was a chocolate and jam factory, buzzing with workers producing confectionary. Now you're more likely to find the space jammed with locals, students and tourists who gather for Roasted Brown espresso, homemade fodder and the laid-back vibe.

TIP GET YOUR CHOPS AROUND THE (VEGAN) ARTICHOKE SOURDOUGH SANDWICH

With bags of space, plenty of comfy chairs, benches and tables, it's a great spot to grab brunch with the gang. Crowd-pleasers like the house granola topped with maple syrup, mixed seeds, berries and greek yogurt, and the super-stuffed breakfast ciabatta are the perfect antidote to a big night out in Dublin.

The team behind Blas know how to throw a cracking knees up and the roomy cafe can be personalised for launch parties, wedding celebrations and corporate events.

ESTABLISHED
2014

KEY ROASTER
Roasted Brown
Roasters +
Makers

BREWING METHOD
Espresso

MACHINE
La Marzocco
Linea

GRINDER
Anfim

OPENING HOURS
Mon-Fri 8am-4pm
Sat-Sun 10am-4pm

 Gluten FREE

 BEANS AVAILABLE INSTORE

 WIFI

 DISABLED ACCESS

---

www.blascafe.ie T: 01 8736022

 f @blascafe @blascafe @blascafe

MAP № 43 CAMERINO BAKERY

158 Capel Street, Dublin 1

If the eight *McKennas' Guide* plaques adorning the walls don't confirm the quality of this Dublin bakery, the lengthy queue of locals lining up for their daily coffee and carb fix certainly proves its status as one of the city's finest food stops.

A window of toothsome treats tempts the uninitiated inside to a counter heaving with funked-up brownies, bejewelled flapjacks and dainty cupcakes. Everything is baked each morning by founder Caryna Camerino and her crew of talented bakers, and it's wise to cash in on the seasonal specials as they're often gone by 1pm.

TIP SWING BY THE NEW OUTPOST AT MERRION SQUARE FOR MORE SWEET THRILLS

The itsy-bitsy size of the kitchen-cafe means it's a take-out only situation when it comes to the Roasted Brown espresso. Pick up a challah roll stuffed with rotisserie chicken plus a silky flat white and head to the riverside for an epic lunch break.

Inspired to improve your baking skills? Check out the vegan baking and mini bakers workshops, as well as the private lessons.

ESTABLISHED
2014

KEY ROASTER
Roasted Brown Roasters + Makers

BREWING METHOD
Espresso

MACHINE
La Marzocco Linea PB

GRINDER
Anfim

OPENING HOURS
Mon-Fri **7.30**am-**5**pm
Sat **11**am-**4.30**pm

 Gluten FREE

 BEANS AVAILABLE INSTORE

 WIFI

 DISABLED ACCESS

 BRING YOUR OWN Cup

 DOG FRIENDLY

www.camerino.ie   T: 01 5377755

f @camerinobakery   @camerinobakery   @camerinobakery

MAP№ 44 TANG

9a Lower Abbey Street, Dublin 1

Tang's industrial-chic decor lures customers with the promise of creative food and excellent coffee. Retaining the top spot in TripAdvisor's Dublin restaurant rankings is no mean feat, but locals and visitors consistently give it the thumbs up.

You'll know it's your lucky day if you bag a window stool looking out onto bustling Abbey Street. Choose your caffeine black, white or iced from the pleasingly pared-back menu. There's no over-complicated prep here: immaculately roasted beans from nearby Upside are brewed skilfully and allowed to speak for themselves.

INSIDER'S TIP ALL PACKAGING IS COMPOSTABLE AND CUSTOMERS ARE INCENTIVISED TO REMEMBER THEIR KEEPCUPS

Food takes the best local ingredients and funks them up with a touch of the Mediterranean and Middle East. For breakfast, expect your avo on toast to buzz with spicy salsa and be bejewelled with beetroot hummus and dukkah. Lunch plates are piled high and flatbreads and salads can be customised to be vegan, veggie or meaty. And don't forget to treat yo'self to a sweet bake to finish from the tempting countertop array.

ESTABLISHED
2016

KEY ROASTER
Upside Coffee Roasters

BREWING METHOD
Espresso, batch brew

MACHINE
Nuova Simonelli Aurelia II

GRINDER
Nuova Simonelli Mythos 2

OPENING HOURS
Mon-Fri **7.30**am-**5**pm
Sat **10**am-**4**pm

Gluten FREE

BEANS AVAILABLE INSTORE

WIFI

CYCLE FRIENDLY

DISABLED ACCESS

BRING YOUR OWN Cup

DOG FRIENDLY

www.tang.ie
f @tangdublin @tangfood

№45 COFFEEANGEL IFSC

The Exchange Building, George's Dock, IFSC, Dublin 1

With the help of architect Chris Boyle, coffeepreneurs Karl Purdy and Caroline Sleiman have created a sleek collection of speciality coffee houses which typify the Coffeeangel brand without conforming to identikit cafe culture.

Each of the five Dublin outposts has been designed with its unique location in mind and the latest venue, in the heart of the financial district, is a pared-back compilation of walnut-stained plywood, clean lines and bold typography. Grab a seat at the window and watch the business world rush by while you savour the milk chocolate and redcurrant notes of the house espresso blend.

PICK UP SINGLE ORIGIN COFFEES FROM THE RETAIL SHELVES AND TAKE THE GOOD VIBES HOME

Coffeeangel has been at the forefront of speciality in Ireland for 15 years and is now embracing the industry's next – sustainable – chapter. Its #YourCupOurFuture campaign has already saved over 25,000 single-use cups from going to landfill and raised around €5,000 for Friends of the Earth Ireland.

ESTABLISHED
2004

KEY ROASTER
Bailies Coffee Roasters

BREWING METHOD
Espresso, filter, pourover

MACHINE
La Marzocco

GRINDER
Mythos One, Mahlkonig EK43,

OPENING HOURS
Mon-Fri 7am-5pm
Sat 9am-4pm

 Gluten FREE

 BEANS AVAILABLE INSTORE

 WIFI

 DISABLED ACCESS

 BRING YOUR OWN Cup

www.coffeeangel.com T: 01 5241030

f @coffeeangel 🐦 @coffeeangel 📷 @coffeeangel

MAP №46 INDIGO & CLOTH

9 Essex Street, East Temple Bar, Dublin 2

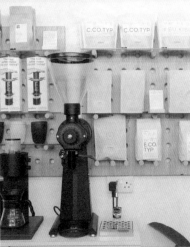

If you're after an unusual setting in which to experience speciality coffee, this minimalist spot on the ground floor of Indigo & Cloth is one for your hit list.

The menswear and design shop has hosted a concession cafe alongside its curation of clothes from up-and-coming designers since 2015, but owner Andy Collins took the operation in-house at the start of 2019.

INSIDER'S TIP
DRINK-IN COFFEE IS SERVED WITH A GLASS OF STILL OR SPARKLING FILTERED WATER

The relaunched coffee bar now mirrors the clothing store and releases a seasonal menu of beans (spring/summer, autumn/winter), plus a select collection of pastries and small bites. The line-up makes good use of the new Marco SP9 and features around seven options on filter, alongside two espressos (one from Bailies and an international guest).

Design-savvy home brewers should bring spare change as the cafe also stocks a range of gorgeous ceramics and statement brewing pieces, as well as locally made artisan food products.

ESTABLISHED
2015

KEY ROASTER
Bailies Coffee Roasters

BREWING METHOD
Espresso, Marco SP9 filter

MACHINE
La Marzocco Linea PB

GRINDER
Mahlkonig EK43, Mazzer Major, Mythos One

OPENING HOURS
Mon-Fri 9am-6pm
Sat 10am-6pm
Sun 11am-6pm

Gluten FREE

BEANS AVAILABLE
INSTORE

WIFI

CYCLE FRIENDLY

OUTDOOR SEATING

DISABLED ACCESS

BRING YOUR OWN Cup

DOG FRIENDLY

www.indigoandcloth.com T: 01 6706403
f @indigoandcloth @indigoandcloth @indigoandcloth

MAP 47 BEAR MARKET COFFEE

3 South Great George's Street, Dublin 2

The youngest Bear Market cub has inherited all the edgy design, welcome-home warmth and exceptional coffee that its indie brothers are known for.

Sinuous and sculptural decor with hand-built furniture and warming copper accents is modern – but not painfully so. This is still a spot where locals seek sanctuary for a good brew with something sweet on the side.

Colombia and Guatemala meet head on in Bear Market's house blend and only 100 per cent organic beans are invited to the party. Silverskin take care of roasting duties, while guests round out a menu that's designed to help customers expand their coffee horizons.

 TIP LEARN HOW TO BREW LIKE A PRO WITH A BEAR MARKET ONLINE TUTORIAL

Espresso, pourover and immersion coffee is the main draw, although there is also a stack of cakes and pastries to tide over rumbling tums. Purists can pick a buttery croissant from the heaped counter while the weak willed may find themselves led astray by a cruffin.

ESTABLISHED
2018

KEY ROASTER
Silverskin Coffee Roasters

BREWING METHOD
Espresso, filter, V60, AeroPress

MACHINE
La Marzocco Strada

GRINDER
Mahlkonig EK43, Nuova Simonelli Mythos One

OPENING HOURS
Mon-Fri **7.30**am-**7**pm
Sat **8**am-**7**pm
Sun **11**am-**6**pm

 Gluten FREE

 BEANS AVAILABLE INSTORE

 WIFI

 DISABLED ACCESS

 BRING YOUR OWN Cup

www.bearmarket.ie

 @bearmarketcoffee @bearmarketco @bearmrktcoffee

MAP №48 SHOE LANE COFFEE – TARA STREET

7 Tara Street, Dublin 2

The decor at this cosy hangout may reference its cobbler shop heritage, however it is finely crafted coffee, not handmade footwear, which now draws the crowds.

Hints of its former guise – a Singer sewing machine and shoe lasts – are interspersed with contemporary bare-bulb light fittings and salvaged timber, and the result is a space packed with quirky character.

Beans brewed via V60, batch and espresso are sourced from local roastery Full Circle and, if your caffeine levels are already at their peak, plump for the Swiss-water decaf blend.

TIP THE OUTSIDE BENCH IS A GREAT PEOPLE-WATCHING SPOT ON SUNNY DAYS

In summer, beans are slow-extracted in chilled water for 12-14 hours in order to concoct the homemade cold brew.

Disco Fridays welcome the weekend in style; a mini glitter ball and boppy tunes pep up the pre-work coffee run.

ESTABLISHED
2016

KEY ROASTER
Full Circle Roasters

BREWING METHOD
Espresso, batch filter, V60, cold brew

MACHINE
La Marzocco Linea PB Auto Brew Ratio

GRINDER
Mythos One Clima Pro

OPENING HOURS
Mon-Fri 6.30am-6.30pm
Sat 8am-6pm
Sun 10am-4pm

 Gluten FREE
 BEANS AVAILABLE INSTORE
 WIFI
 CYCLE FRIENDLY
 OUTDOOR seating
DISABLED ACCESS
BRING YOUR OWN cup
 DOG FRIENDLY

www.shoelanecoffee.ie T: 01 6779471
f @shoelanecoffee @shoelanecoffee

№ 49 À TABLE

40 Forbes Quay, Forbes Street, Dublin 2

L ocated in Dublin's thrumming Docklands, À Table ticks all the boxes required of a buzzy neighbourhood spot. Cracking coffee? Check. Outside seating with views to the river? Check. Hearty and healthy bites to set you up for the day? Double check.

The coffee menu focuses on doing the classics impeccably, with Bailies beans providing an exceptional espresso. A monthly rotating filter is brewed by french press and, if you're looking for something out of the ordinary to get you firing on all cylinders, there are guests from the likes of Girls Who Grind.

TIP ALMOND CROISSANTS (BAKED BY FIREHOUSE) SELL OUT BEFORE YOU CAN SAY 'MAKE MINE A ...'

Passing on something to eat at À Table is risky business: the honest-to-goodness Irish breakfast is not to be underestimated, while lunch offers imaginative dishes with international flavours and plenty of veggie, vegan and gluten-free possibilities. Online ordering lets you skip the lunchtime queue, and late opening hours on Wednesdays and Thursdays call for post-work cheese, wine and small plates.

ESTABLISHED
2016

KEY ROASTER
Bailies Coffee Roasters

BREWING METHOD
Espresso, french press

MACHINE
La Marzocco GB5

GRINDER
Victoria Arduino Mythos One

OPENING HOURS
Mon-Tue, Fri
7.45am-**4**pm
Wed-Thu **7.45**am-**8**pm
Sat **9.30**am-**4**pm
Sun **10.30**am-**4**pm

 Gluten FREE

 BEANS AVAILABLE INSTORE

 WIFI

 OUTDOOR seating

 DISABLED ACCESS

 BRING YOUR OWN cup

 DOG FRIENDLY

www.atable.ie   T: 01 4458970
f @atablecafe   @ @atablecafe

DEVELOPED WITH BARISTAS FOR BARISTAS

- Perfect for latte art
- No added sugar
- Cholesterol free, low fat alternative to milk
- 30% less calories than skimmed & regular soy milk

Baristas know their coffee better than anyone. That's why we got baristas to help us make our new, low calorie Almond Breeze® Barista Blend. It's deliciously creamy and frothy, making it perfect for the world's finest coffee. And because it's an almond drink, it's dairy free and soya free

For more information & stockists visit **bluediamondalmonds.co.uk**

MAP № 50 EBB & FLOW COFFEE

56 Clontarf Road, Dublin 3

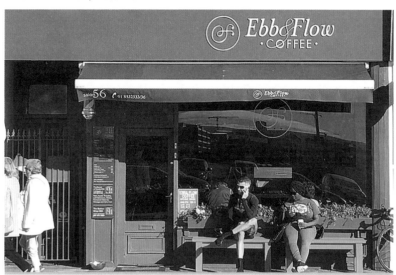

From dialing in the latest batch of beans each morning to sourcing milk from local producers and fashioning the perfect latte art, consistency is king at this Clontarf Road coffee shop.

To ensure that speciality standards continue to soar, Ebb & Flow founders Dave Smyth and Fiona Fitzgerald have enlisted the help of Full Circle. The Dublin roastery stocks the trio of grinders with a knockout espresso and fortifies the offering with regularly updated seasonal finds.

 THE CAFE IS SUPER DOG-FRIENDLY AND VISITING PUPS OFTEN MAKE IT ONTO THE HOUSE INSTAGRAM

If you've time to kill, ask the baristas for their roast recommendation for pourover and pair your filter with something carby from the menu of toasties. Then chill on the bench out front as you savour your picks.

Early birds can fuel up for a busy day in Dublin with hearty porridge bowls topped with almond flakes, banana chips or pumpkin seeds.

ESTABLISHED
2015

KEY ROASTER
Full Circle
Roasters

BREWING METHOD
Espresso,
pourover

MACHINE
La Marzocco
Linea Classic

GRINDER
Mythos One x 2,
Mahlkonig EK43

OPENING HOURS
Mon-Fri **7.30**am-**5**pm
Sat **8**am-**5**pm
Sun **9**am-**5**pm

 Gluten FREE

 BEANS AVAILABLE — INSTORE

 WIFI

 OUTDOOR SEATING

 BRING YOUR OWN cup

 DOG FRIENDLY

www.ebbandflow.ie   T: 087 9699884

f @ebbflowcoffee   @ @ebbflowcoffee

№ 51 HAPPY OUT CAFE

Bull Wall, Bull Island, Dublin 3

There aren't many spots where you can sip a freshly pulled single origin espresso to the sound of waves lapping the shore – and even fewer located just 15 minutes from Dublin city centre.

Stroll along Clontarf seafront, hop over The Wooden Bridge and wander down Bull Wall to discover the island's caffeinated oasis, Happy Out. The coffee and toastie bar was built by uncle and nephew duo Brian Hanratty and Karl McCullagh and is housed within a souped-up shipping container.

TIP SEIZE THE DAY: DROP BY EARLY FOR AN ESPRESSO AND BREKKIE OF OVERNIGHT OATS

Seaside frolickers, wildlife enthusiasts and watersports junkies flock to the friendly hangout to recharge with a Roasted Brown flat white and one of the signature sandwiches – the 'asparagorgeous' (roasted asparagus, red pepper, mushroom, spinach, cream cheese and three cheeses) is the current veggie fave.

A guest coffee – always single origin – from the house roaster showcases some of the diversity of flavours to be discovered.

ESTABLISHED
2017

KEY ROASTER
Roasted Brown
Roasters +
Makers

BREWING METHOD
Espresso

MACHINE
La Marzocco
Linea PB

GRINDER
Nuova Simonelli
Mythos One

OPENING HOURS
Winter 9am-4.30pm
Summer 9am-7.30pm

MAP 52 HONEY HONEY

Strand Road, Portmarnock, Dublin 13

I f it's a come-in-and-make-yourself-at-home welcome and a stonkingly good cup of coffee that you're after, a visit to Honey Honey hits the sweet spot. Rosy-cheeked walkers, straight from strolling along Portmarnock's Velvet Strand, mingle with the locals at this effortlessly cheery cafe.

The super friendly team skilfully concoct brews using beans from Bailies in Belfast, a collaboration between the two resulting in a perfectly balanced (and ethically sourced) house blend. Guest roasts from Galway's Calendar Coffee fly the flag for seasonality.

TIP PAIR YOUR COFFEE WITH A CHILLI AND FENNEL SAUSAGE ROLL

A newcomer to Dublin's coffee scene, the cafe has already attracted accolades, while innovations such as the daily vegan soup keep the regulars returning.

Breakfast and lunch is served Monday to Friday, but weekends are given over to all-day brunching. Choose the spicy eggs with chilli jam, chased with a strong espresso to kickstart Saturday morning in style.

ESTABLISHED
2018

KEY ROASTER
Bailies Coffee Roasters

BREWING METHOD
Espresso

MACHINE
Astoria Sabrina

GRINDER
Mahlkonig K30

OPENING HOURS
Mon-Fri **7.30**am-**4**pm
Sat **9**am-**5**pm
Sun **10**am-**4**pm

www.honeyhoneycafe.com T: 087 9160072

f @honeyhoneycafe @honeyhoney_cafe

MAP № 53 CRACKED NUT
71 Camden Street, Dublin 2

It's no surprise that they've cracked the coffee at this trendy Camden Street cafe, as co-proprietor Dave Smyth not only set up Ebb & Flow Coffee in Clontarf, he also co-owns Full Circle Roastery.

Discerning caffeine fiends gather here for organic and ethically-sourced beans served as espresso or V60, safe in the knowledge that they're imbibing an ultra-fresh roast. The coffee travels down the road from the roastery at Grantham Place.

TIP GO TO WORK ON AN EGG POT: SCRAMBLED EGGS SERVED WITH SOURDOUGH, AVOCADO AND KALE

Since taking over in February 2018, Dave and Louise have also set about cracking the food and vibe. A bright and light refurb encourages banter over brunch offerings such as Buddha bowls of warm sushi rice, carrot and cabbage pickle and seasonal greens.

Follow smug-face-inducing healthy fare with an almond croissant or peanut butter brownie topped with roasted peanut caramel praline. It's all about balance, right?

ESTABLISHED
2018

KEY ROASTER
Full Circle Roasters

BREWING METHOD
Espresso, V60

MACHINE
La Marzocco FB80

GRINDER
Anfim Super Caimano

OPENING HOURS
Mon-Fri 7.30am-4pm
Sat 9am-3pm

www.crackednut.ie   T: 087 9699884
f @crackednutdublin   @crackednut

ᴹᴬᴾ 54 FIRST DRAFT COFFEE & WINE

34 Lennox Street, Portobello, Dublin 8

The first draft is the starting point for any good creation, and the various evolutions of this Dublin stalwart have seen it undergo repeated refinement.

After an unexpected move to new digs in Portobello last year, First Draft's latest incarnation is a foray into evening service. Founder Ger O'Donohoe is as passionate about low-intervention wine as he is about speciality coffee, and extended opening hours have enabled him and the small team to introduce a curated collection of organic bottles and small plates.

Coffee is served all day and Roasted Brown continues to supply the neighbourhood hub with County Wicklow roasted beans. There's usually a guest on filter too.

 PICK UP BEANS AND BOTTLES TO-GO FROM THE RETAIL SELECTION

Daytime passes at a leisurely pace here, so take the opportunity to sit among the house plants and get started on the first draft of that masterpiece you've been mulling over. Evenings are more lively – and the perfect remedy for any case of writer's block.

ESTABLISHED
2016

KEY ROASTER
Roasted Brown Roasters + Makers

BREWING METHOD
Espresso, Kalita Wave, Chemex, Wilfa batch brew

MACHINE
Nuova Simonelli Aurelia II

GRINDER
Anfim

OPENING HOURS
Mon-Tue **8**am-**3**pm
Wed-Fri **8**am-**10**pm
Sat-Sun **9**am-**10**pm

www.firstdraftcoffeeandwine.com T: 086 8604517

f @firstdraftcoffee 🐦 @1stdraftcoffee @ @firstdraftcoffeeandwine

MAP 55 TWO FIFTY SQUARE

10 Williams Park, Lower Rathmines Road, Dublin 6

The spirit of Melbourne has taken root in Rathmines, thanks to Two Fifty Square.

The cafe's location might be off the main drag (and a long way from Oz), but Dublin bean geeks have sniffed it out. A peek through the picture windows into the industrial-chic interior reveals baristas hard at work serving caffeine-hungry hordes.

TIP ESPRESSO LOVERS WILL APPRECIATE THE ROTATING MENU OF SEASONAL ROASTS

The coffee comes exclusively from Two Fifty's award winning roastery and only single estates make the cut, so every cup is one of distinction.

Brewing methods range from espresso (via the Sanremo Cafe Racer) through to V60 and AeroPress, while chilled refreshment comes in the form of cold brew and iced options.

As Two Fifty Square's coffee has built a loyal following, so has its brunch menu. Comfort food plays a big role and Spanish baked eggs, maple and bacon pancakes, and rib-eye steak all receive star billing.

ESTABLISHED
2014

KEY ROASTER
Two Fifty Square
Coffee Roasters

BREWING METHOD
Espresso,
V60, AeroPress,
cold brew

MACHINE
Sanremo Cafe
Racer

GRINDER
Mahlkonig EK43,
Mythos One
Clima Pro

OPENING HOURS
Mon-Fri 8am-6pm
Sat-Sun 9am-6pm

Gluten FREE

BEANS AVAILABLE
INSTORE

WIFI

CYCLE FRIENDLY

OUTDOOR Seating

DISABLED & ACCESS

BRING YOUR OWN Cup

COFFEE COURSES

DOG FRIENDLY

www.twofiftysquare.ie   T: 01 4968336

f @twofiftysquarecoffee   @250squarecoffee   @250squarecoffee

MAP 56 PROJECT BLACK

3 Ranelagh, Dublin 6

Passengers spilling from Ranelagh Station don't know how lucky they are – few commuters are blessed with small-batch speciality coffee of this quality on their morning journey.

The tiny cafe is an offshoot of Two Fifty Square, a mini coffee empire that's blossoming across Dublin. Allegiance to the mother-roaster means that high grade single-origin beans, meticulously roasted just ten minutes away, figure in every brew served from the on-street hatch.

 COOL DOWN WITH A REFRESHING ICED VIETNAMESE COFFEE OR AN ICED MATCHA

Project Black's red-brick exterior is all rough-hewn shabby but, inside, things are slickly modern. A slab-of-marble counter contrasts with black tiles as glossy as the coffee dripping through the V60s, while a gleaming Sanremo Opera squeezes out espresso in style.

Thanks to the Two Fifty barista school, the Project Black team are well versed in delivering consistently ace coffee. If you've time to watch them at work, head inside and treat yourself to a melty doorstop toastie.

ESTABLISHED
2017

KEY ROASTER
Two Fifty Square
Coffee Roasters

BREWING METHOD
Espresso, V60,
AeroPress

MACHINE
Sanremo Opera

GRINDER
Mahlkonig EK43,
Sanremo SR50

OPENING HOURS
Mon-Fri 7am-5.30pm
Sat-Sun 8am-5.30pm

 Gluten FREE

 BEANS AVAILABLE INSTORE

 WIFI

 OUTDOOR seating

 DISABLED ACCESS

 BRING YOUR OWN cup

www.twofiftysquare.ie T: 01 5672110
f @projectblackd6 🐦 @projectblackd6 📷 @projectblackd6

MAP № 57 SHOE LANE COFFEE – DUN LAOGHAIRE

Dun Laoghaire Shopping Centre, George's Street Upper, Dun Laoghaire, Co. Dublin, A96 DK81

Shoe Lane welcomed a second shop to the family in winter 2018 when founders Jane Lunnon and Jonathan Hughes launched this sister venue in the seasidey suburb of Dun Laoghaire.

The new space has quickly garnered a good rep with the locals for its simple hot food menu and carefully brewed speciality coffee. House roaster Full Circle has come along on the coastal jolly and its Dublin-bronzed beans stock the Mythos grinder.

A simplified coffee line-up filters out the faff of choosing your drink, and most punters can find their perfect accompaniment in the four-strong alt-milk line-up which includes Oatly and Bonsoy.

TIP INSIDER'S **FOR SWEET SHORESIDE SIPPING, TRY THE YUZU ICED ESPRESSO TONIC**

On the food front, vegan and veggie options, sourdough toasties (try the triple cheese) and gourmet sausage rolls hit the spot after a seaside stroll.

Grab a stool at the window bench and watch the world go by or take your brew (in a customised reusable) for a jaunt around the harbour.

ESTABLISHED
2018

KEY ROASTER
Full Circle
Roasters

BREWING METHOD
Espresso, V60,
batch brew,
cold brew

MACHINE
La Marzocco
Linea PB Auto
Brew Ratio

GRINDER
Mythos One
Clima Pro

OPENING HOURS
Mon–Fri **6.30**am–**6.30**pm
Sat **8**am–**6**pm
Sun **10**am–**4**pm

www.shoelanecoffee.ie   T: 01 5162182

f @shoelanecoffee   @ @shoelanecoffee

MAP 58 URBUN CAFE

Old Bray Road, Cabinteely, Dublin 18

If the lip-smackingly delicious sight of the homebaked soda bread, brownies and lemon drizzle lined up on the cake bar isn't enough to make you linger, the proposition of freshly roasted free-range chicken served in crusty bread should do the trick.

Scrumptious ingredients are used to good effect in Urbun's popular piri piri chicken with red cabbage 'slaw on ciabatta – just one of the many specialities on a menu crammed with locally sourced goodies.

TIP TRY THE BLUEBERRY BUTTERMILK PANCAKES WITH MACADAMIA BRITTLE AND CRÈME FRAÎCHE

However, it's not just the extensive brekkie, brunch and lunch offering that entices locals to hang out at the industrial-chic Cabinteely cafe: the team's long-established relationship with Fermoy roaster Badger & Dodo means you can be assured of a stellar espresso, courtesy of the Blackwater blend.

If you're feeling adventurous, avail yourself of the barista's weekly choice of single origin – perfect paired with a berry scone.

ESTABLISHED
2011

KEY ROASTER
Badger & Dodo
Boutique Coffee
Roasters

BREWING METHOD
Espresso

MACHINE
La Marzocco
Linea

GRINDER
Nuova Simonelli
Mythos

OPENING HOURS
Mon-Fri 8am-5pm
Sat-Sun 10am-5pm

 Gluten FREE

 BEANS AVAILABLE INSTORE

 WIFI

 CYCLE FRIENDLY

 BRING YOUR OWN Cup

---

www.urbun.ie T: 01 2848872

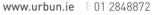 @urbun @urbuncafe @urbuncafe

DUBLIN
ROASTERIES

MAP № 59 UPSIDE COFFEE ROASTERS

Unit 14, Chart House Business Park, 157-159 Richmond Road, Fairview, Dublin 3

A t Upside, Jamie O'Neill and team adhere to the mantra that 'the quality is found in the detail', so they're always refining their sourcing and tweaking roast profiles to create sweet, balanced and complex coffees.

It's reaping rewards, as the number of cafes and businesses discovering their ever-changing selection of seasonal origins is steadily growing.

'THE QUALITY IS FOUND IN THE DETAIL'

Quality beans are only half of the story, however, as the team are also on a mission to forge even better relationships with their wholesale customers by ever-improving their training programme and providing ongoing support.

Home brewers are looked after via the website which sells sweet Central and South American coffees for espresso and milk-based drinks, as well as exciting new beans from East Africa and Asia. There are usually six coffees and a decaf on offer, depending on seasonality.

ESTABLISHED
2016

ROASTER
MAKE & SIZE
Mill City Roaster
15kg

OPEN
BY APPOINTMENT

BEANS
AVAILABLE
ONLINE ONSITE

---

www.upsidecoffee.com T: 085 1624966

f @upsidecoffeeroasters 🐦 @upside_coffee 📷 @upside_coffee

MAP № 60 FULL CIRCLE ROASTERS

2 Grantham Place, Dublin 8

From Full Circle's swanky roastery south of central Dublin, freshly roasted beans travel to lucky baristas and home brewers across the city and beyond.

The past year has seen the burgeoning roasting team move to a new facility and upgrade their kit, reflecting the onwards-and-upwards ambition of David Smyth and Brian Birdy's 2014 startup.

Beans are mindfully sourced from across the globe and given a distinctly personal treatment: roasting is all done by hand, as is bagging, tagging and dispatch. Quality and consistency are top priority for the Full Circle crew and that demands obsessive attention to detail.

'EVERY MONDAY, ROASTING IS FOLLOWED BY A QUALITY-CONTROL CUPPING SESSION'

Using a 12kg Probat Probatone offers batch-size flexibility and, as only the finest seasonal beans are used, year-round deliciousness is assured. Every Monday, roasting is followed by a quality-control cupping session to ensure everything's up to scratch.

Barista training is also on offer from the coffee-obsessed team.

ESTABLISHED
2014

ROASTER
MAKE & SIZE
Probat
Probatone 12kg

OPEN
BY APPOINTMENT

COFFEE
COURSES

BEANS
AVAILABLE

---

www.fullcircleroasters.ie   T: 087 9699884

f @fcroaster 🐦 @fcroaster 📷 @fcroaster

MAP №61 TWO FIFTY SQUARE COFFEE ROASTERS

11 Rathfarnham Road, Terenure, Dublin 6

Since 2014, Two Fifty Square has built its rep as a not-to-be-underestimated force in Irish coffee. And rightly so, given its commitment to meticulous sourcing and bronzing of the finest speciality beans at its state-of-the-art Terenure roastery.

Africa and Central and South America are TFS's preferred bean-hunting grounds. The team truffle out award winning harvests, trading directly in the pursuit of small batches for the new roastery – at least six origins are available at any time.

'TWO FIFTY SQUARE'S TASTEBUDS HAVE PUNISHINGLY HIGH STANDARDS'

Each coffee is first tried out on the 2.4kg sample roaster before full-scale roasting takes place on the 15kg or 60kg machines. Each roast then faces stringent cupping tests – TFS tastebuds have punishingly high standards.

To ensure the coffee tastes as good as the day it left the roastery, the crew also run a barista school and provide equipment for cafe customers. For the real deal, sample the latest lot at one of their two Dublin cafes.

ESTABLISHED
2014

ROASTER
MAKE & SIZE
60kg
15kg
2.4kg profile roaster

CAFE
ONSITE

OPEN
BY APPOINTMENT

COFFEE
COURSES

BEANS
AVAILABLE
ONLINE   ONSITE

---

www.twofiftysquare.ie   T: 01 4904953

f @twofiftysquarecoffee   🐦 @250squarecoffee   📷 @250squarecoffee

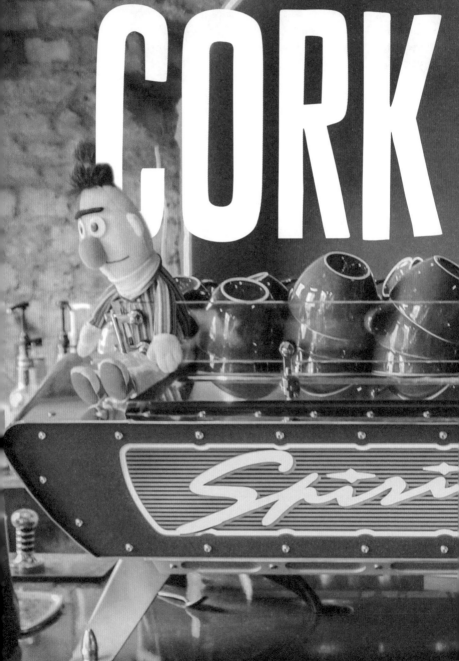

N°62
LAB 82 COFFEE

⬡ CAFES

⬡ ROASTERIES

All locations are approximate

Lower Glanmire Rd

River Lee

N8

R852

St Michael's Dr

CITY GATE

R852

MAP 62 LAB 82 COFFEE

82 Lower Glanmire Road, Victorian Quarter, Cork, Co. Cork, T23 TK20

Since September 2018, commuters and sightseers passing through Cork's Kent Station have been able to punctuate their journey with the sweet full-bodied punch of a Brazilian espresso or the fruity uplift of a Rwandan or Ethiopian filter.

However, mid-trip perk-me-ups from Amsterdam's White Label roastery aren't the only thing brightening the day at this friendly cafe. Brunch dishes such as eggs benedict or a full Irish entice a steady stream of visitors from 8am, while the lure of guest coffees from Cork's The Golden Bean or a decaf from Tipperary's The Old Barracks bliss out the bean buffs 'til 6pm.

INSIDER'S TIP CAN YOU QUACK IT? SPOT THE 30 DUCKS HIDDEN AROUND THE CAFE

A daily-changing dessert offering makes Insta moments inevitable. Subject your friends to a severe case of FOMO with the likes of cookie ice cream sandwiches, raspberry ripple buttercream cupcakes, Cornetto pancakes and 15 different types of brownie.

ESTABLISHED
2018

KEY ROASTER
White Label Coffee

BREWING METHOD
Espresso, filter

MACHINE
Kees van der Westen Spirit Triplette

GRINDER
Mahlkonig EK43, Mazzer Kony x 3

OPENING HOURS
Mon-Sat **8**am-**6**pm
Sun **10**am-**5**pm

Gluten FREE

BEANS AVAILABLE — INSTORE

WIFI

OUTDOOR SEATING

DISABLED ACCESS

---

www.lab82coffee.com   T: 085 8370000

f @lab82coffee   🐦 @lab82coffee   📷 @lab82coffee

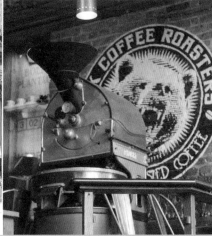

MAP 63 CORK COFFEE ROASTERS

2 Bridge Street, Cork, Co. Cork, T23 PY7H

S mall but mighty is the best description of this iconic Cork cafe. Owners John and Anna Gowan imbue their cosy coffee hub with the same good vibes and passion they felt 11 years ago when they opened the doors to delighted speciality seekers.

Their mission now, as then, is to roast and serve great coffee. It's a calling that's seen them set up their own Cork roastery, launch a second cafe on French Church Street and hatch a plan to open a third on Anglesea Street later this year.

TIP CHECK OUT THE REGULAR ART EXHIBITIONS AND BARISTA TRAINING COURSES

Each of their convivial cafes is a place to chat with friends, old and new, over a rich Rebel blend espresso and a buttery pastry, scone or tart.

'Our neighbourhood locations attract people of all ages and from all walks of life so you never know who you might meet,' says Anna.

Try one of the new guest coffees, imported and roasted by the crew (of course), and don't forget to buy a bag of your fave on the way out.

ESTABLISHED
2008

KEY ROASTER
Cork Coffee Roasters

BREWING METHOD
Espresso, filter, drip

MACHINE
La Marzocco

GRINDER
Mahlkonig

OPENING HOURS
Mon-Fri
7.30am-**6.30**pm
Sat **8**am-**6.30**pm
Sun **9**am-**5**pm

 Gluten FREE

 BEANS AVAILABLE INSTORE

 WIFI

 CYCLE FRIENDLY

 OUTDOOR Seating

 BRING YOUR OWN Cup

 COFFEE COURSES

www.corkcoffeeroasters.ie   T: 021 7319158

f @corkcoffee   🐦 @cork_coffee   @ @corkcoffeeroasters

MAP 64 DUKES COFFEE COMPANY – CAREY'S LANE

4 Carey's Lane, Cork, Co. Cork

Dukes was one of the first to champion speciality in Cork and, since 2004, has fuelled the city's caffeine folk from this former coffee warehouse in the Huguenot Quarter.

Locality is at the core of Dukes' philosophy and at its flagship outpost (you'll find another at City Gate) you can imbibe beans from regional roasteries and chow down on dishes prepared from local produce.

Instead of pledging allegiance to one roast, the team switch up the espresso blend every fortnight, giving regular customers the chance to explore Ireland's game-changing roasteries. There are usually a number of guest options too.

INSIDER'S TIP THE CREW ALSO PACK PICNIC BOXES TO ACCOMPANY TAKE-OUT COFFEES

Dukes' reputation as Cork's best brekkie draws the crowds while the brunch menu (try the homemade potato cakes with scrambled eggs and smoked salmon) lures late risers. There's also a new health-conscious line-up of lighter options if you're set on squeezing in a slice of cake after lunch.

ESTABLISHED
2004

KEY ROASTER
Multiple roasters

BREWING METHOD
Espresso, V60, Chemex

MACHINE
La Marzocco Linea Classic

GRINDER
Mahlkonig K30

OPENING HOURS
Mon-Sat 8am-5pm
Sun 10am-5pm

www.dukes.ie   T: 021 4905877

f @dukescoffeecork   🐦 @dukescoffeeco   📷 @dukes_coffee_co

MAP 65 SOMA COFFEE COMPANY

23 Tuckey Street, Cork, Co. Cork, T12 WD98

Stripped back industrial-style decor puts coffee front and centre at this Cork cafe-roastery. And since taking the roasting operation in-house last year, team Soma have been crafting caffeine deserving of the spotlight.

Only beans that score 85 or higher on the speciality scale (anything over 80 hits SCA standards) are carefully bronzed on the sky-blue Giesen before every drop of flavour is extracted at the brew bar.

 THE INDIVIDUALLY DESIGNED COFFEE BAGS ARE BECOMING SOUGHT-AFTER COLLECTABLES

The life of a Soma bean is an access-all-areas affair: visitors can watch the roasters working on the next batch in the Tuckey Street space and read the cupping scores which are printed on the retail bags. And if you've any gaps in your knowledge, the enthusiastic baristas are very happy to help.

High standards also extend to the weekend brunch and midweek lunch line-up; swing by for spicy corn and feta salsa with poached eggs, toasted sourdough and hollandaise.

ESTABLISHED
2017

KEY ROASTER
Soma Coffee Company

BREWING METHOD
Espresso, V60, AeroPress, Chemex, batch brew, cold brew

MACHINE
Rancilio Speciality RS1

GRINDER
Mahlkonig Vario, Mahlkonig Tanzania

OPENING HOURS
Mon-Fri **7.30**am-**7**pm
Sat **9**am-**7**pm
Sun **10**am-**6**pm

 Gluten FREE

 BEANS AVAILABLE INSTORE

 WIFI

CYCLE FRIENDLY

OUTDOOR Seating

DISABLED ACCESS

BRING YOUR OWN Cup.

 DOG FRIENDLY

www.somacoffeecompany.ie   T: 086 6660938

f @somacoffeecompany   @somacoffeecoltd   @somacoffeecompany

MAP 66 THREE FOOLS COFFEE

Kiosk 2, Grand Parade, Cork, Co. Cork, T12 X967

Many coffee businesses talk about the importance of transparency, but few are housed in an actual glass box in the middle of a busy city.

Floor-to-ceiling windows give passersby a peek at the caffeine alchemy going down at Three Fools, before tempting them in to sample the speciality coffee and high quality snacky food (which includes plenty of plant-based and gluten-free options).

This year the team are enthusing about the micro-lots of beans they're brewing, which have been sourced from farms in Brazil, Rwanda and Ethiopia. They're keen to introduce new and interesting coffees to the seasonal selection, so a lot of time is spent tracking down and tasting fresh finds.

INSIDER TIP: SNAP UP THE COLD BREW DURING THE BRIEF MOMENT THAT IS IRISH SUMMERTIME

Three Fools' Ethiopian Boji made it to the 2019 Irish Brewers Cup where barista Alex Cregan picked up second place with the natural-process coffee. The team are keen to share their knowledge, so head over to learn a few tricks of the trade at one of the free brewing masterclasses.

ESTABLISHED
2015

KEY ROASTER
Three Fools Coffee

BREWING METHOD
Espresso, filter, V60, Chemex, cold brew

MACHINE
BFC Aviator

GRINDER
La Marzocco Vulcano x 2, Mahlkonig EK43

OPENING HOURS
Mon-Fri 8am-6pm
Sat 9am-6pm
Sun 11am-6pm

www.threefoolscoffee.ie

f @threefoolscoffee 🐦 @3foolscoffee ◎ @threefoolscoffee

MAP 67 FILTER ESPRESSO AND BREW BAR

19 George's Quay, Cork, Co. Cork

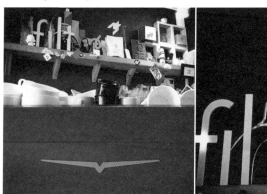

The diminutive size of this Cork speciality shop is entirely inverse to the quality and variety of coffee experiences to be discovered within its four walls.

Hosting an ever-growing roster of beans from big and little (local and international) roasters, Filter founder Eoin Mac Carthy has created a haven for intrepid and experimental coffee followers.

The crack team of baristas are passionate about their craft so, whether you're exploring something fruity via woodneck or sticking with velvety espresso, they'll fashion you a mighty fine coffee. With up to 20 beans available at any time (yes, really – look for the plethora of jars behind the brew bar), it's worth picking the crew's brains for a seasonal recommendation.

 COUNTER BAKES TO PAIR WITH YOUR BREW INCLUDE MONSTER FRUIT-STUDDED SCONES

If you're craving something familiar, the main roasts from Third Floor and Cloud Picker are stalwarts. 3FE's natural Brazilian Passeio roast is also a house fave for its lip-smackingly good milk chocolate, fudge and pecan notes.

ESTABLISHED
2012

KEY ROASTER
Multiple roasters

BREWING METHOD
Espresso, Chemex, Kinto, V60, AeroPress, Kalita Wave, Clever Dripper, Hario Woodneck

MACHINE
Victoria Arduino Black Eagle

GRINDER
Mahlkonig Vario, Mythos One

OPENING HOURS
Mon-Fri
7.30am-5.30pm
Sat 9am-5pm
Sun 10am-3pm

 Gluten FREE

 BEANS AVAILABLE INSTORE

 WIFI

 CYCLE FRIENDLY

 OUTDOOR SEATING

 BRING YOUR OWN CUP

 COFFEE COURSES

 DOG FRIENDLY

www.filter.ie T 087 3924479

f @FILTER @filtercork @filter_espresso_and_brew_bar

68 THE BOOKSHELF COFFEE HOUSE

Unit 5, The Elysian, Eglinton Street, Cork, Co. Cork

There's a dish to please even the fussiest bruncher at this slick all-day eatery: want something on toast? You've got it. Huevos rancheros? Sí. Breakfast pizza? Now we're talking ...

The lively team ensure that breakfast at The Bookshelf runs easy like Sunday morning. A creative bunch of cooks whip up all sorts of deliciousness in the kitchen while a small army of baristas do their thang behind the bar, resulting in a crowd-pleasing pairing of brewology and gastronomy.

TIP INSIDER'S SAMPLE THE BOOKSHELF MARTINI WHICH IS SPIKED WITH HOMEMADE COLD BREW

In keeping with the cafe's pared-back European style, coffee is sourced from The Barn. The Berlin outfit delivers a lighter roast in its small-batch beans which yield standout flavours when sampled on V60, Chemex or batch brew. The guest coffee spot also roams the continent – recent roasters include Munich's Man Versus Machine.

Come Friday, the spot morphs into a buzzy evening hangout where revellers clash forks over sharing plates and swap cappuccinos for house cocktails.

ESTABLISHED
2012

KEY ROASTER
The Barn

BREWING METHOD
Espresso,
V60, Chemex,
batch brew

MACHINE
Victoria Arduino
Black Eagle
Gravitech

GRINDER
Mythos One

OPENING HOURS
Mon-Thu
7.30am-**5**pm
Fri **7.30**am-**10**pm
Sat **9**am-**10**pm
Sun **9**am-**5**pm

Gluten FREE

BEANS AVAILABLE
INSTORE

WIFI

DISABLED ACCESS

BRING YOUR OWN *Cup*

www.bookshelfcoffee.com T: 021 4311591
f @thebookshelfcoffeehouse @thebookshelfcoffee

MAP 69 DUKES COFFEE COMPANY – CITY GATE

The Plaza, City Gate, Mahon, Cork, Co. Cork

Tech types and worker bees reroute their morning commute to pass Dukes' City Gate outpost so, pre-9am, expect to join the throng of laptop-wielding professionals seeking their daily caffeine fix.

It's not just Cork's coffee-to-go crew who make tracks to the modern cafe in the heart of the IT district. With bags of space and a first floor co-working area, it's also a favourite with visiting coffee geeks and those in need of a little time out of the office.

TIP GORGEOUS DAY? CHILL ON THE TERRACE WITH A COLD BREW – IT'S A PEOPLE-WATCHING PARADISE

A rotating line-up of guest roasters keeps the creative ideas flowing, and regional names such as West Cork Coffee and 3FE often headline. If you've time to spare, ask the baristas what's good on filter.

Bowls of vibrant homemade salads, seasonal wraps and freshly baked sausage rolls are also available if more than just caffeine is required to fuel your afternoon.

In summer, stop by on Wednesdays and Fridays for the cookouts on the deck, then feast like a lunch-break king on slow-cooked brisket and chargrilled fish.

ESTABLISHED
2008

KEY ROASTER
Multiple roasters

BREWING METHOD
Espresso, filter, cold brew

MACHINE
La Marzocco FB80

GRINDER
Mahlkonig K30 twin

OPENING HOURS
Mon-Fri 7.30am-5pm

www.dukes.ie   T: 021 4350139

f @dukescoffeecork   🐦 @dukescoffeeco   @dukes_coffee_co

CORK
ROASTERIES

MAP 70 CORK COFFEE ROASTERS

2 French Church Street, Cork, Co. Cork, T12 E94K

The adage of 'keeping it simple' has certainly helped this Cork coffee roastery to flourish.

Founder John Gowan uses a classic 1930s cast-iron coffee roaster (which he lovingly maintains) to ensure that the flavours locked within his pick of high-altitude green beans are gently developed with care. And, by knowing the foibles of this vintage beauty, he can subtly adjust the roast to ensure each bean exhibits its optimum aroma and flavour profile.

ESTABLISHED
2005

ROASTER
MAKE & SIZE
Vintage
cast-iron 22kg,
Probat

OPEN
BY APPOINTMENT

COFFEE COURSES

BEANS AVAILABLE
ONLINE / ONSITE

'JOHN AND WIFE ANNA PLAN TO OPEN A THIRD CAFE IN CORK THIS YEAR FEATURING A DEDICATED TRAINING FACILITY'

It's this traditional way of working that customers, new and old, seem to appreciate. The family-owned business has experienced an increasing demand for its freshly roasted small-batch beans – from coffee lovers and wholesale customers alike – with a similar uptake in barista courses and cafe consultations. So much so that John and wife Anna plan to open a third cafe in Cork this year, which will also feature a dedicated training facility.

www.corkcoffeeroasters.ie   T: 021 4678010

f @corkcoffee   🐦 @cork_coffee   ⊙ @corkcoffeeroasters

MORE GOOD
COFFEE SHOPS &
ROASTERIES

MORE GOOD
COFFEE SHOPS
MORE EXCEPTIONAL PLACES TO DRINK COFFEE ...

71

3FE – GRAND CANAL STREET

32 Grand Canal Street Lower, Dublin 2
www.3fe.com

72

5A

5a Lockview Road, Belfast, BT9 5FH

73

BABUSHKA KITCHEN CAFE

South Pier, Portrush, Co. Antrim, BT56 8DQ
www.babushkakitchencafe.co.uk

74

BADGER & DODO

Fairgreen Road, Galway, Co. Galway
www.badgeranddodo.ie

75

BEAR MARKET COFFEE – BLACKROCK

19 Main Street, Blackrock, Co. Dublin
www.bearmarket.ie

76

BEAR MARKET COFFEE – GEORGE'S QUAY

Unit 2, Westblock, George's Quay, Dublin 1
www.bearmarket.ie

77

BEAR MARKET COFFEE – PEMBROKE STREET

1a Pembroke Street Lower, Dublin 2
www.bearmarket.ie

78

BODEN PARK COFFEE COMPANY

317 Ormeau Road, Belfast, BT7 3GB
www.bodenparkcoffeeco.com

79

BRIDEWELL COFFEE & PROVISIONS

19 High Street, Donaghadee,
Co. Down, BT21 0AH

80

CARGO COFFEE

16c Belfast Road, Bangor,
Co. Down, BT20 3PX

81

COFFEE CULTURE

55 South King Street, Dublin 2
www.coffeeculture.ie

82

COFFEE WORKS

Unit 2, Griffeen View, Lucan, Co. Dublin
www.coffeeworks.ie

83

CORK COFFEE ROASTERS – FRENCH CHURCH STREET

2 French Church Street, Cork, Co. Cork
www.corkcoffeeroasters.ie

84

DISTRICT

469 Lisburn Road, Belfast, BT9 7EZ
www.districtcoffee.co.uk

85

DUBLIN BARISTA SCHOOL

19a Anne Street South, Dublin 2
www.dublinbaristaschool.ie

86

GENERAL MERCHANTS CAFE

361 Ormeau Road, Belfast, BT7 3GL
www.generalmerchants.co.uk

87

LEGIT COFFEE CO

1 Meath Mart, 24 Meath Street,
The Liberties, Dublin 8
www.legitcoffeeco.com

88

LOVE SUPREME

57 Manor Street, Stoneybatter, Dublin 7
www.lovesupreme.ie

89

MEET ME IN THE MORNING

50 Pleasants Street, Portobello, Dublin 8
www.mmim.ie

90

NECTAR COFFEE

26 Parnell Place, Cork, Co. Cork

91
OH! DONUTS
55 Upper Arthur Street, Belfast, BT1 4HG
www.ohdonuts.co.uk

92
ROOT & BRANCH COFFEE SHOP AND BREW BAR
Ormeau Baths, 18 Ormeau Avenue, Belfast, BT2 8HS
www.rootandbranch.coffee

93
STORYBOARD
Clancy Quay, Islandbridge, Dublin 8
www.storyboardcoffee.com

94
THE HAPPY PEAR
Tower Road, Clondalkin, Dublin 22
www.thehappypear.ie

95
THE POCKET
69 University Road, Belfast, BT7 1NF
www.thepocket.coffee

96
TWO PUPS COFFEE
74 Francis Street, Dublin 8

97
VICE COFFEE INC.
Wigwam, 54 Middle Abbey Street, Dublin 1
www.vicecoffeeinc.com

98
WARREN ALLEN COFFEE
15 Maylor Street, Cork, Co. Cork

MORE GOOD
ROASTERIES
ADDITIONAL BEANS FOR YOUR HOME HOPPER

99
3FE

32 Grand Canal Street Lower, Dublin 2
www.3fe.com

100
BADGER & DODO BOUTIQUE COFFEE ROASTERS

Ballynafauna, Fermoy, Co. Cork
www.badgeranddodo.ie

101
BAOBAB COFFEE ROASTERS

The Mill, Celbridge, Co. Kildare
www.baobab.ie

102
CLOUD PICKER

Unit 5, Castleforbes Business Park, Sheriff Street, Dublin 1
www.cloudpickercoffee.ie

103
ROASTED BROWN ROASTERS + MAKERS

Behind Firehouse Bakery, Delgany, Co. Wicklow
www.roastedbrown.com

104
ROOT & BRANCH ROASTERY AND BREW BAR

Unit A3, Portview Trade Centre, 310 Newtownards Road, Belfast, BT41HE
www.rootandbranch.coffee

105
SILVERSKIN COFFEE ROASTERS

Unit 13 Blackwater Road, Dublin Industrial Estate, Dublin 11
www.silverskincoffee.ie

106
STONE VALLEY COFFEE ROASTERS

35 Ashe Street, Clonakilty, Co. Cork
www.stonevalleyroasters.com

107
THE HAPPY PEAR COFFEE ROASTERS

Kilcoole Industrial Estate, Creowan Road, Kilcoole, Co. Wicklow, A63 D276
www.thehappypear.ie

108
THE STUDIO COFFEE ROASTERS

The Narroways, Bettystown, Co. Meath
www.thestudiocoffee.com

MEET OUR COMMITTEE

The *Independent Coffee Guide*'s committee is made up of a small band of leading coffee experts and the team at Salt, who work with Ireland's coffee community to produce the guide

JAMES SHEPHERD

James has worked in the coffee industry for 16 years and currently holds the role of European account executive at Specialty Coffee Association (SCA). After starting his career with a leading UK roaster in 2002, James relocated to Dublin in 2006. He's competed in the Scottish Barista Championships and UK finals twice, and also judges in the UKBC, IBC and WBC (also MCing at the latter).

KARL PURDY

Coffeeangel, Karl's group of Dublin coffee shops, celebrates its 15th anniversary this year. *The Irish Times* named him '*the father of the Irish speciality scene*' and his progressive approach to coffee and customer service has seen Coffeeangel grow to include five locations across the city.

KARL

JAMES

CELESTE OWENS

Originally hailing from Australia, Celeste has been working in coffee in the UK for seven years. In her role as barista and sales consultant at Bailies Coffee Roasters, she's passionate about making speciality more widely accessible and encouraging more people to drink sustainably and ethically sourced coffee. When she's not promoting the speciality scene, she likes collecting house plants, making ceramics and listening to true-crime podcasts.

GER O'DONOHOE

Ger is a passionate educator and career barista from Dublin. His company, First Draft Coffee, opened its doors six years ago and has earned an enviable reputation as a seat of coffee excellence in Ireland.

Last year Ger relocated his cafe and training space to Portobello and extended the opening hours to introduce a menu of low-intervention wines and small plates.

EOIN MAC CARTHY

Eoin has been working in cafes for over two decades, launching Filter with partner Alex O'Callaghan in 2012. The coffee-obsessive barista made the switch from mainstream coffee culture to speciality nine years ago and collaborates with local and international roasters to bring a globetrotting array of phenomenal beans to his diminutive Cork coffee bar.

CELESTE

GER

EOIN

COFFEE
NOTES

SOMEWHERE TO SAVE DETAILS OF SPECIFIC BREWS
AND BEANS YOU'VE ENJOYED

COFFEE NOTES

SOMEWHERE TO SAVE DETAILS OF SPECIFIC BREWS
AND BEANS YOU'VE ENJOYED

INDEX